PRIDE
OF THE
LIONS

PRIDE
OF THE
LIONS

THE BIOGRAPHY
OF
JOE PATERNO

Frank Fitzpatrick

TRIUMPH
BOOKS

Library of Congress Cataloging-in-Publication Data

Fitzpatrick, Frank.
  Pride of the Lions : the biography of Joe Paterno / Frank Fitzpatrick.
    p. cm.
  Includes bibliographical references.
  ISBN 978-1-60078-615-0
  1. Paterno, Joe, 1926– 2. Football coaches—United States—Biography. 3. Pennsylvania State University—Football—History. 4. Penn State Nittany Lions (Football team)—History. I. Title.
  GV939.P37F58 2011
  796.332092—dc23
  [B]
                                                                          2011025248

This book is available in quantity at special discounts for your group or organization. For further information, contact:

Triumph Books
542 South Dearborn Street
Suite 750
Chicago, Illinois 60605
(312) 939–3330
Fax (312) 663–3557
www.triumphbooks.com

Printed in U.S.A.
ISBN: 978-1-60078-615-0
Design by Sue Knopf

All photos courtesy of AP Images unless otherwise specified.

For Dillon and Jaina

CONTENTS

Introduction

Several years after i'd finished a 2004 book on the coach and his program, Joe Paterno asked a colleague what had become of me. "Where's the kid who wrote the book?" he inquired. "The kid" was near 60 at the time. When you are, like Paterno, 84 and entering your 62nd season on Penn State's football staff, the world is full of kids. The winningest coach in big-time football history has outlived, outlasted, and outcoached all of his rivals, not to mention most of those who have chronicled his achievements.

Entering this 2011 season, his 46th as the Nittany Lions head coach, Paterno's familiar black mane is mostly gray. His gait has slowed, not by choice but because of injuries he suffered along the sideline and in practice. He has made some concessions to his staff but not to time. His active mind remains that of a young man's, even if his cranky impatience increasingly betrays his age.

He has won 401 football games at Penn State, including a record 24 bowls. He has had two national champions and five unbeaten seasons. What else is there? Why does he go on? When will he retire?

Those questions lurk behind any late-life examination of Paterno and his admirable legacy of triumph on and off the field. In his more than six decades, he has avoided even the hint of a major scandal, has graduated a disproportionately large percentage of his players, and has managed to fill enormous Beaver Stadium Saturday after Saturday. And whether or not you want to debate how much of the credit belongs to him, the only common denominator through those years of Penn State glory has been Paterno. Long past the age when others might have quit, content in their accomplishments, the idealistic Paterno soldiers on, convinced that he is fulfilling the fate life set before him.

He is, like Penn State football, veiled from too-close scrutiny—by geography, inclination, and habit. In the author's note to the previous book, I began by pointing out how difficult it was to write about Paterno and Penn State football, "[It's] a lot like being a linebacker defending against one of those sweeps his Nittany Lions love to run: You've got to keep your head up at all times, fight off wave after wave of interference, and never take your eyes off the target, no matter how well-protected and untouchable he might seem." By attempting to do so again, I found a man and a story that are among the most remarkable in post–World War II America.

With a better understanding of the Penn State football environment, by supplementing my earlier research and observation with additional reading, by frequent visits to the archives at a Penn State library that bears Paterno's name, by new interviews and a reliance on decades of work by generations of my sportswriting colleagues, I hope I've scraped away a few layers of Paterno's famously tanned skin.

This project would have been inconceivable without all the books, magazines, newspapers, and documents listed in the bibliography. Particularly helpful were the oral-history materials gathered by Penn State historian Lou Prato and *Altoona Mirror* writers Neil Rudel and Cory Giger, and an earlier Paterno biography, *No Ordinary Joe*, by Michael O'Brien. Wherever possible, I tried to use the fruits of my own research and interviews. But I depended often on comments he made to others over the years—at news conferences, in private interviews, and during radio and TV broadcasts.

The result, I hope, is an entertaining narrative of Paterno's life with an emphasis on those moments that helped transform this football coach from Brooklyn into a beloved and often misunderstood American icon.

1

COLLEGE FOOTBALL IN ALABAMA is a religious experience, one with rituals, a liturgy, and a deity in a hound's-tooth hat. "The definition of an atheist in Alabama," longtime University of Georgia coach Wally Butts once said, "is someone who doesn't believe in Bear Bryant." So it was hardly surprising that several hours before their team's 2010 opener against visiting Penn State thousands of crimson-clad Alabama fans reverently lined a pathway outside Bryant-Denny Stadium in Tuscaloosa.

These zealots were securing spots along the Walk of Champions, 100 yards of brick connecting University Boulevard and the stadium's north entrance. Since its construction six years ago, Alabama supporters have gathered there early on football Saturdays. Lining the walk, they not only can glimpse visiting players as they arrive but, more importantly, they can welcome the home team in the same adoring way Christ was welcomed to Jerusalem.

As if to enhance the spiritual connection between 'Bama boosters and their team, the university recently added a shrine in an adjacent plaza. There, the four former Alabama coaches who had produced national championships—Gene Stallings, Frank Thomas, Wallace Wade, and Paul "Bear" Bryant—were honored like secular saints, their bronze statues standing in well-tended grottos that invited silent worship.

Such manufactured venues for veneration were typical of major college football in the 21st Century. For its few dozen behemoths—and Alabama and Penn State were surely among them—the sport was a wildly successful amalgam of salesmanship, spectacle, and spirituality. These two state schools, for example, spent a combined $51 million on football in 2009 and earned $146 million, each filling their constantly expanding stadiums with more than 100,000 spectators on autumn Saturdays. And it was the unwavering devotion of financial supporters, true believers large and small, that paid the bills. Bonding rites like the Walk of Champions and the coaches' shrine helped ensure that the money would keep flowing. After all, if you failed to buy a personal-seat license, what would the Bear think?

On this sweltering September afternoon, the waiting spectators—men in garish crimson blazers and perfectly coiffed women in neat dresses of the same hue—seemed more expectant than usual. The Alabama team they prepared to greet had won a national title the previous January, the school's 13th, and was predicted to contend for another. But on September 11, 2010, there was an added attraction. They were going to get a peek at a football god. Not some bronzed idol in a grotto, but one who at 83 was still walking, breathing…and astonishingly, coaching.

Joe Paterno, "St. Joe" as he often was called by fans and his few detractors, was making his first trip to Alabama in 20 years. For weeks, sportswriters and columnists in the state had been heralding the return. Paterno's connections to and admiration for Bryant lent him a special cachet here. As noted by Buck Paolone, a former Penn State player who lives near Tuscaloosa, his former coach was "admired, respected, and talked about in the most reverent of terms [by Alabama's football fans]. Not in the same terms as Bear Bryant, but damn near close."

Each season it got more difficult to grasp the Methuselah-like span of Paterno's career. He had been at Penn State since 1950. Consumer credit cards didn't exist then, and fewer than a million American homes had televisions. Amos Alonzo Stagg was still coaching. Jim Thorpe was still alive. And Bear Bryant, dead now for 27 years, was just 36 years old.

Paterno waited 16 years to become a head coach. His first game, in 1966, came against a Maryland team coached by Lou Saban. Saban, who moved on from Maryland to coach at eight more places, had died in 2009, 30 years after his final game at a Division I school.

Today, 526 games later, Paterno's coaching opponent was another Saban. Alabama's Nick, 58 now, had been just 14 years old when Lou, a much older cousin, faced Penn State in 1966.

In the interim, Paterno had accumulated more wins than any coach in major-college history. No one had more bowl appearances, more bowl victories, more seasons as a head coach, or more seasons at a single school. He had raised millions, donated millions, and won countless honors. He even had his own statue in a grotto outside Beaver Stadium at State College.

Penn State's buses arrived outside the stadium first, disgorging players who looked surprisingly young and small in street clothes so ill-fitting they made the famously fussy Paterno cringe. When the old coach emerged, his appearance sparked a buzz along the Walk of Champions. Soon respectful applause and a rhythmic chant of "Joe Pa-Ter-No" erupted.

If any of these Alabamans were getting their first look at him, it must have been disappointing. Physically, even in his prime, Paterno never matched the conventional image of a football coach. He was more bird than Bear. He didn't loom; he flitted and fidgeted. Still a trim 165 pounds, there was none of the bulk-gone-to-beefiness of a Charlie Weis or a John Madden, none of the visible intensity of a Jon Gruden or a Pete Carroll, none of the clever gambler's bearing that Bryant possessed in spades.

Instead what Paterno had after all these years was an aura. The Nittany Lions' coach had accumulated so much agreeable history that it glowed like a halo above a head that was at long last graying. That past insulated him from criticism. It guaranteed him control. It preceded him like a path of palm fronds into visiting cities and made him an icon in his adopted state. It earned him fame, fortune, power, and respect.

He could quell whatever doubts arose about his health or his supposedly fading abilities by pointing to the past and summoning some strategy or trick he had used before. He could deflect disapproval by citing a name, a year, a team that emphasized his career's remarkable success. He'd heard it all, accomplished it all, seen it all. He could do anything it seemed… except walk away.

Thick glasses—however, thanks to recent Lasik surgery that helped correct 20/20,000 vision, not as thick as he has worn in the past—covered dark and purposeful eyes. His olive skin was tanned from vacations at the New Jersey shore and practices in the hot Central Pennsylvania sun. His lips were pursed and his face was locked in a perpetual squint that lent it an inquisitiveness.

Bespectacled, slight, and swarthy, Paterno not only looked different than most coaches, he was different. He spoke differently, thought differently, had different interests. How many successful college coaches majored in literature at an Ivy League university? Or talked about Dante at a news conference?

Or gave their future wives a copy of Camus' *The Stranger*, asking her to write a summary of her thoughts on the book so that he could compare them with his own? Or listened to opera while devising plays? Perfectly happy to inhabit the public's image, Paterno once confessed, "I am a little bit of an egghead."

That dichotomy—a kind of renaissance man thriving in a profession with an inherent anti-intellectual strain—was just one of the many Paterno contradictions. A streetwise kid from teeming Brooklyn, he had spent the bulk of his life in a small, bucolic Pennsylvania mountain town. A coach who saw football as a means to a fuller life, not an end in itself, Paterno was consumed by the game. "He doesn't like the travel," said Guido D'Elia, a Penn State marketing and communications official who is Paterno's liaison to the outside world. "He wastes no time. No matter what city we're in, New York or Washington, the second we can get back, we're gone."

What had drawn him to the profession against the wishes of his proud mother was his competitive spirit. What made him stay so long was his idealism. Despite his reputation, he was more idealistic than intellectual. The Jesuits had convinced him early that men were born with destinies. Long ago he learned that his destiny was coaching at Penn State. Proud of his status as not just a head coach but a fully tenured professor, content in a town so small it would barely have qualified as a neighborhood in his native Brooklyn, he had stubbornly remained in Happy Valley, spurning numerous offers from the NFL and elsewhere, as well as a few entreaties to run for political office.

In Pennsylvania, he had won two national championships, had five unbeaten seasons, and operated a program that had never been on NCAA probation. Penn State's reputation was so pristine, in fact, that even the hard-probing *Dallas Morning*

News had to admit it was "as clean a program as can be found." Somehow, Paterno had learned to balance what his late brother termed his "rage to win" with a belief that it was more essential to build character than Hall of Fame credentials.

Not long after winning his first national championship in 1982, Paterno urged his university to capitalize on the title not by building new sports facilities or hiring more coaches, but by improving the faculty. "Without Joe, Penn State might still be an agricultural college," said Ronnie Christ, a Harrisburg sportswriter who has known Paterno for decades.

Paterno has never been afraid to espouse his Grand Experiment—his long-held notion that football and academics could be compatible. In making that point, he has lectured CEOs, trustees, graduates, players, and fellow coaches. Some have welcomed the advice. Many, particularly his more pragmatic coaching colleagues, have not. While they respected Paterno, they frequently found his pronouncements to be sanctimonious, holier-than-thou, and even condescending.

He was certainly the most recognizable coach in college sports. But was he the best? How would such a thing be determined? By victories? Years on the job? Graduation rates? Bobby Bowden, Paterno's vanquished longtime rival for most career wins, said whatever the ground rules, it was no contest. "When you add up the three main criteria for a successful football program—academic success, football success, and development of character—Joe wins by a landslide," Bowden said.

Because he has lingered so long, Paterno has already outlived many of those who canonized him over the years, the ones for whom his Grand Experiment was fresh and appealing and possible. A new generation of broadcasters and sportswriters was not so worshipful. For them, time had tattered the image.

They were as likely to see Paterno as a stubborn octogenarian as a saint.

They were not entirely wrong. For at least a decade now, Paterno had been the sporting symbol of a cranky old man too cantankerous to yield to reality. The more he aged, the sharper his faults appeared. Increasingly prickly with the media, officials, his players, and his assistants, Paterno could seem demanding, dictatorial, petty, annoying.

He had evolved from ambitious prodigy to coaching genius to elder statesman to an impossibly aged legend. Some of the younger fans along the Walk of Champions who knew him only in that last stage couldn't contain their smiles and giggles. People their age snickered whenever Paterno yelled at an official or a sportswriter, garbled a name, or tried to talk about some new technology. He once called Twitter "Tweedle-Dee" and Facebook "Face Mask."

For all his accomplishments, he has remained nearly devoid of pretensions. "He always, always wants to stay in the background," said son Jay, a PSU assistant. He drives an old car, lives in a modest house, and belongs to no country clubs.

Villanova basketball coach Jay Wright likes to tell the story of his first meeting with the Pennsylvania legend. With a mutual friend who had promised an introduction, Wright had arrived at the Penn State coach's home after a rain-soaked Nittany Lions victory in 2007. He was ushered into the den. Soon Paterno, shoes off, still wearing his wet sideline clothing, shuffled in. He told Wright to grab a beer from a nearby cooler and a seat in his recliner. The then 80-year-old coach sat down on the floor, propping his back against the paneled wall. "I couldn't believe it," said Wright, who grew up near Philadelphia as a Penn State fan. "This was Joe Paterno. An idol of mine. He was soaked and shoeless. Sitting against a wall. He had one chair in his family room, and he gave it to me."

Wearing a pressed and dry version of the same outfit—khakis, a buttoned-down blue oxford shirt, blue-striped tie, a blue windbreaker, and familiar black cleats—he averted his eyes downward as he moved through the cheering Alabama throng. Cell phones and cameras were pointed at him. His pipe-cleaner-thin legs bowed, and he walked with a slight limp.

A violent sideline collision with a player in 2006 had broken Paterno's left leg. Two years later he had badly injured the other while he was, in one of the many archaic phrases he still used, "horsing around" at practice. In recent years, he also was hospitalized briefly for fatigue and dehydration and had hip-replacement surgery. For a while, his gait was so unsteady and the concern for his well-being so intense that he had to use a cane and coach from the press box.

After each of those injuries, and as recently as the past summer when digestive problems forced him to cancel several annual preseason events, speculation arose that Paterno at last was ready to step aside. Such talk had popped up sporadically over the last 20 years, particularly when Penn State endured an unprecedented run of losses around the turn of the millennium. And when it wasn't fans, alumni, and the media suggesting he soon retire, it was Paterno himself. "Every five years or so," said his son Jay, "he says he's gonna get out in a couple of years." But here he was, on the doorstep of his 61st season at Penn State, his 45th as its head football coach, still on the job. He might not have been quite as involved in the details as he once had been, but to anyone close to his program it remained obvious that the man who already was in college football's Hall of Fame was no figurehead.

Once inside the Alabama stadium, Paterno strolled slowly around the lush playing field, like an old soldier revisiting a battlefield from his youth. He was no sentimentalist, but he had to realize he wouldn't be back to this college football landmark. Alabama was coming to Penn State in 2011 and after that, who knew? College schedules were made years, sometimes decades, in advance. He had one year remaining on his contract, and at 85 when it expired, he almost certainly would be at the end of the line.

Or would he? Others who had anticipated his departure in the past had been wrong. In 2004 and again in 2008, Paterno had been granted nearly unthinkable extensions, the most recent a three-year deal with a bizarre clause that permitted either side to shorten or extend it "as necessary," though no one doubted Paterno's ultimate authority in the matter.

As plausible as his retirement sounded to outsiders, it wasn't something Paterno seemed willing to face. Not yet. He told some of the high school athletes he recruited in 2011 that he'd be around "five more years." He might never be ready to walk away from the role that had consumed his life. "I've never been around anyone who has aged as reluctantly as Joe," said longtime friend Jim Tarman, the former Penn State sports infrmation director and athletics director.

He stayed because, for him, this was not a job. This was life. This was destiny. He had made the decision he was meant to make in 1950. He was fortunate. "My destiny and what I *wanted* to do," he once said, "were one and the same."

The weeks leading up to this Alabama game had given Paterno opportunities for reflection. Not that he was a particularly reflective man. You didn't thrive for as long as he had by looking back. Even now, in his ninth decade on earth, he preferred to gaze ahead. He'd changed and adapted whenever he'd needed to while at the same time keeping intact the things he felt were important, such as Penn State's plain uniforms and his rigid practice routines. But he was 83. And even if he preferred not to think about it or discuss it whenever he was asked by sportswriters who were insistent in raising the subject no matter how much he demurred, he had to know he couldn't go on forever.

As the sun began to fall behind the stadium, the temperature stayed near his age. Paterno, inexplicably, wouldn't shed his jacket. The blue nylon zip-up, imprinted with a Penn State logo and a Nike swoosh, had replaced a sports coat as his favored sideline attire. He could have removed it. That, however, would have disturbed the routine, the order he'd so carefully nurtured.

There was a significance to everything he did, everything he wore. His was a uniform that, in his mind at least, made a statement about a well-run, purposeful program, just as the neat Yankees pinstripes did the first time he saw them in person as a high schooler in the 1940s. He was no sweat-suit coach. Sweat suits implied a casualness about one's mission, and there was nothing casual about what Paterno did.

On this day, hovering all around the octogenarian and as oppressive as the Alabama heat, were two unpleasant reminders of inevitability—fellow coaching legends Bryant and Bowden… one dead, the other discarded.

The massive stadium in which Paterno watched his team warm up bore Bryant's name. So did many other institutions and thoroughfares in this college town 47 miles southwest of Birmingham. Bryant couldn't be avoided here. And if ever an opponent had haunted Paterno, it was Bryant who, with his syrupy drawl, his impeccable style, Southern manners, and gambler's boldness, was Paterno's antithesis. "Self-confidence hung in the air around him like a fine mist," an awestruck Paterno once said of the coach.

Throughout the week preceding the Alabama game, Paterno had been asked often about Bryant. The old coach had resisted talking about his long-deceased rival, more out of unease than respect, it seemed. "Why get into it?" he said.

Not many people had gotten the best of Paterno over the years. Bryant had. When a magazine recently ranked the greatest college football coaches of all time, Paterno finished second to Bryant. The Bear's Alabama teams beat his Nittany Lions in all four head-to-head meetings. One of those, the 1979 Sugar Bowl, was for a national title. Before that game, Bryant appeared on the sideline of the Louisiana Superdome without his trademark hound's-tooth hat. Paterno, already intimidated, wondered what kind of gamesmanship was afoot. So he asked. Bryant said he had removed the hat because he didn't want his mother to see him wearing one indoors. That kind of character, whether invented on the spot or not, impressed the Penn State coach for whom a man's outward appearance mirrored what was inside.

Paterno's Nittany Lions would lose that national title game 14–7. Bryant outfoxed him again, and Paterno was devastated. "Nothing of the kind ever compared to this loss," he would write a decade later. "It got to me. It hammered at my ego. When I stood toe to toe with Bear Bryant, he outcoached me."

What also bothered Paterno about Bryant, though he certainly wouldn't raise the subject here in Alabama, was the way Bryant had operated his program. Once, before a game at State College, Bryant had asked Pennsylvania's governor to dedicate a lane of traffic for the team's bus to travel the 90-plus miles from Harrisburg. Penn State officials, bemused by that kind of benevolent arrogance, were happy the governor said no. Bryant also was one of the first to encamp his teams in players-only dorms, a practice Paterno abhorred. "Maybe Bryant believed in protecting his Red Tide from the mental distractions of a university," Paterno wrote in 1989, "Thank God I wasn't protected that way at Brown, and today I wouldn't for one minute consider segregating my players that way at Penn State."

It was odd that fate had brought Paterno here one more time. More than Bryant's career, it was his death that had been on Paterno's mind for many years, particularly as questions about his own future grew louder and more frequent. The Alabama coach retired in December 1982. Thirty-seven days later on January 26, 1983, Bryant suffered a massive heart attack and died at Tuscaloosa's Druid City Hospital. It was all too painful a reminder for Paterno whose father also had died of a heart attack shortly before his own planned retirement.

The coach would forever see those deaths as cautionary tales. Retire, they suggested, or go without your *raison d'être* for even a month and your life was over. "Retire? Why?" Paterno would say in what became his mantra whenever the unpleasant subject arose. "What am I going to do? Cut the grass?"

Bowden, meanwhile, was alive and well. But his presence must have been equally unnerving. An Alabama native who would be watching his first game as a spectator in more than a half-century, Bowden had been forced out as Florida State's coach that winter, though he was, at 80, three years younger than Paterno. Free to be a fan ("I saw tailgaters!" he excitedly exclaimed to reporters before Penn State–Alabama) but clearly forlorn, the amiable Bowden was a peripatetic museum piece. Before the game, he held a news conference to plug his new book, then roamed the sidelines hugging old friends, sportswriters, state policemen, coaches.

Many of the questions at Bowden's news conference concerned Paterno. Bowden envied his old rival, he said, because as was not the case at Florida State, he apparently was being allowed to decide when to walk away. But, Bowden added, he could sense the angst the Penn State coach must be experiencing. Half a lifetime ago, Bowden recalled, when he was 40, he looked at 53-year-old Texas coach Darrell Royal and couldn't imagine himself working at that advanced age. "But then you sign a new five-year contract and another and then another, and pretty soon you're 60 or 70 or 80," he said. "Joe deserves to step away when Joe decides to step away.... What happened to Joe is what I hoped would happen to me. You know, they came to Joe in 2004, wanted him to retire, wanted him to get out. He said, 'No, I'm not going to do it.' The next year he won the Big Ten, beat us in an Orange Bowl and has been to major bowls ever since."

Because the questions never stopped, or perhaps because he was not yet fully recovered from the summer's illness, Paterno's expression seemed tinged with irritation. Things didn't get any more pleasant for him once the game began. As Alabama dismantled his youthful Penn State team 24–7 in the nationally televised contest, he spent much of the time roaming the sideline, carping, barking, pondering, yielding to the unpleasant reality. Not wearing headphones, he seemed at times helplessly marooned, more relic than coach. His Nittany Lions, so young and inexperienced that he had broken a longstanding policy by allowing a true freshman to start at quarterback, didn't resemble a well-coached team, a Paterno team. Penn State made silly mistakes, which only added to the psychological distress their coach was experiencing.

Afterward, in a tiny conference room beneath the stadium, he was late to a news conference and more annoyed than usual when he got there. When a writer for a Penn State sports newsletter politely noted that he hadn't heard one of the coach's many mumbled and truncated responses, Paterno shot back, "Tough."

After decades when he had played the part to perfection, it was no longer easy being Joe Paterno.

2

All in all, Flatbush is like everything else in New York
and Brooklyn, a hustling, eagerly active city community,
with attractive shops and theatres, with restaurants, schools
and churches, with banks and libraries, and with a certain
mellowness that the old history of the town sheds even over
the towering apartment houses on Ocean Avenue.

—"HISTORY OF FLATBUSH,"
BROOKLYN STANDARD UNION,
AUGUST 27, 1928

THE "MELLOWNESS" the anonymous newspaper writer
identified already was vanishing from Flatbush when Joseph
Vincent Paterno was born there on December 21, 1926. It
would soon be overwhelmed by the hustle and eagerness the
writer also sensed and which would forever afterward be linked
with the teeming Brooklyn neighborhood. Geographically and
spiritually near the borough's heart, Flatbush, as authors Myrna
and Harvey Frommer pointed out in *It Happened in Brooklyn*,
would be renowned as "scrappy, tough, and boisterous."

Founded by the Dutch in the 17th Century and originally
called Vlackebos, or "flat woodland," the area was for its first

two centuries a sedate community of farmhouses and handsome Victorian homes occupied by prosperous, largely Protestant merchants.

By the 1920s, it had been energized and transformed through an influx of middle- and working-class families drawn there by the era's increased immigration and a revolution in transportation. New York's rapidly expanding subway system and the construction of the Brooklyn and Williamsburg bridges had made for remarkably easy access, opening the borough to commuters, the upwardly mobile, and even new European immigrants.

Five different trolley lines crisscrossed Flatbush. And the citizens who constantly dodged the clamorous vehicles inadvertently provided a nickname for the borough's National League baseball team, which since 1913 had played its home games in the neighborhood's shrine, Ebbets Field.

The frenetic activity of Manhattan's Lower East Side was transplanted there, though refitted with a more respectable veneer. The *New York Times* described the commercial hustle at the intersection of Fulton Street and Flatbush Avenue, the heart of the neighborhood, as rivaling that of Times Square.

Loehmann's opened the first of its discount department stores just off Flatbush Avenue in the 1920s. Sears & Roebuck soon followed. By the start of World War II, there would be 500 businesses in a 1½-mile stretch along the bustling thoroughfare— butchers, fish mongers, bakers, grocers, tailors, dry-goods and hardware stores, cafeterias, restaurants, and bookstores. Movie theaters like the Flatbush, Paramount, Fox, Albemarle, RKO Kenmore, and the grand 3,000-seat Loew's King provided an outlet for residents who found themselves with more free time.

There were other leisure-time options, too. For most residents, it was just a short walk to the Brooklyn Museum on Eastern Parkway. Prospect Park, the lush urban retreat designed by Frederick Law Olmstead and Calvert Vaux, sat like a green jewel at one end of Flatbush Avenue. And the Dodgers, whose constant striving and repeated futility lent them a colorful national reputation that mirrored the borough's, played 77 home games a year in Ebbets Field, which had been adopted by Flatbush even though it technically resided in adjacent Crown Heights.

Jewish, Irish, and Italian families—many of them recent arrivals from crowded Manhattan tenements—filled Flatbush's homes and apartments. By the time Paterno was born there, demand for housing was so great and available land so scarce that developers had begun to look skyward, constructing enormous six-story apartment buildings along Ocean Avenue and elsewhere.

The Depression would make home ownership a luxury and, like many Brooklyn families, the Paternos rented and switched addresses often, occupying dwellings on Homecrest Avenue, 18th Street, 23rd Street, and 26th Street, all within a narrow geographical range.

You had to keep moving in Flatbush. According to author Nedda Allbray in *Flatbush: The Heart of Brooklyn*, it was the "quintessential urban place." And all that urban living implied in the first half of the 20th Century was on display.

Young children played in the streets, on the sidewalks, on the stoops, and even occasionally on rooftops. Teenagers poured in and out of brooding Erasmus Hall, the looming neo-Gothic high school on Flatbush Avenue. Women bargained noisily with merchants, window-shopped, and chattered with neighbors as they hung clothes, pushed baby carriages, and lugged metal carts or thick paper bags laden with groceries. Men congregated in cigar shops and taverns. At the bustling subway stations, like the one on East 16th Street, elevated trains rumbled to a halt, disgorged carfuls of humanity, and then refilled, day and night.

Residents argued, discussed, and cursed in a cacophony of Yiddish, Italian, and Irish-accented English, the constant babble accompanied by sirens and car horns, police whistles, and the shouts of vendors, newsboys, and children. Al Davis was from Flatbush. So was Leona Helmsley. You had to be loud, persistent, brash, and smart to thrive there. Joe Paterno would become all of those things.

So powerfully would his Brooklyn upbringing shape him that when he was 82, after having lived in rural Pennsylvania for nearly six decades, Paterno would still say, "I'm a New Yorker. I'll always be a New Yorker." He never lost the accent. He never lost the attitude. He rarely avoided a confrontation. He wasn't afraid to step on toes. His tastes remained urbane, choosing books and opera over Central Pennsylvania's popular pastimes, hunting and country music.

While the public Paterno's upright reputation may have helped obscure the rough edges of his Flatbush upbringing, he would never be mistaken for a Pennsylvanian. For all of Happy Valley's supposed charms and transformative powers, the area never purged the Brooklyn from Paterno.

Most of the coach's character derived from his childhood and adolescence. It isn't necessary to wonder if it was nature or nurture that molded him, or whether he took after his mother or father. Paterno absorbed the best of it all—the feistiness of Brooklyn without the arrogance, the virtues of an altruistic father without his willingness to compromise, and the drive of an ambitious mother without her pretensions.

His parents, whose families and personalities were polar opposites, were the children of immigrants. His grandparents were among the 4 million Italians—the vast majority from that nation's chronically poor southern region and Sicily—who had come to the great cities of America's Northeast between 1880–1914.

Paterno's birth precipitated one of the few occasions when his father, Angelo Lafayette "Pat" Paterno, exercised any authority over his wife. The mother had hoped to name the boy in her husband's honor, Angelo Lafayette Jr. But Angelo didn't want to saddle the child with a name that was both overtly ethnic and somewhat pompous. The infant instead would bear two fine Anglicized Italian names: Joseph Vincent. "[It was] one of the few arguments that my gentle dad ever won over my mother's powerful will," Paterno noted.

Angelo—friends and family called him "Pat," short for Paterno—was a careful and determined man, one who earned his high school, college, and law degrees as an adult. He encouraged education in his children, provoking discussion and debate and often leaving books around the house, knowing his curious oldest son would find and devour them. He would instill in the future coach a hunger for knowledge, a sense of fair play, and in an era of ethnic balkanization, a tolerance for others.

So diverse, at least for that era, were the religions and cultures of Flatbush that residents had to learn to hate or tolerate. Many chose the latter option and, by the standards of pre-World War II America anyway, an unusually strong spirit of acceptance developed there.

"The corridor of Flatbush Avenue had suddenly found itself at the crossroads of several beliefs, ideologies, and cultures," author Nedda Allbray wrote, "[that it became] a place where cultures could happily collide."

Angelo Paterno was certainly an exemplar of that spirit. By 1945, he had become the director of an organization called the Interfaith Movement, which was devoted to breaking down racial, ethnic, and religious barriers. That October, just months after the world was first exposed to the horrors of Nazi concentration camps, he delivered a speech during the group's annual banquet at Manhattan's Barbizon Plaza Hotel.

"We must preach to our fellow men, night and day, of the evils of this hydrated monster of bigotry," he said. "The forces of intolerance and hate are on the march today. The seed of hate and discord is being sown all around us. It is our task to inculcate our worthy ideals into the warped minds of the weakling before this seed takes root.... Let me urge you who are assembled here this evening to rededicate your lives to the proposition that all of the forces of intolerance must be expunged from our midst and that you will become a crusader in this most worthy cause."

Born on September 1, 1897, the son of a barber who had emigrated from an Albanian village in southern Italy's Cosenza region—at the instep of the boot—Angelo was the second of seven children. The Paterno name, interestingly enough, translates to "fatherly" or "paternal," and the family was well-educated, idealistic, and more cerebral than the prevailing stereotype of the hand-waving, emotional Italian. Several Paternos of his father's generation would go on to careers as lawyers, educators, and corporate executives.

A high school dropout at 17, Angelo enlisted in the U.S. Army and would become a sergeant. His first son always proudly noted that, under the command of Gen. John "Black Jack" Pershing, Angelo "chased Pancho Villa all over Mexico." But

Angelo also took part in some heavy fighting during World War I, particularly at the Meuse-Argonne.

Angelo returned to Brooklyn after the war, got his high school degree, and was married in 1925. He eventually took a job as a clerk in the Appellate Division of the New York Supreme Court, which whetted his appetite for the law. After his first two children were born, he began attending night classes at St. John's, eventually earning his college and law degrees there.

He loved books and intelligent discussions. Intellectually curious and constantly striving to better his understanding of the world, Angelo kept a dictionary at his side when he read. His children recall his love of opera and the pleasure he took in sitting in his favorite chair listening to the Metropolitan's Saturday afternoon radio broadcasts.

But all was not seriousness. Angelo Paterno was a kidder, someone who enjoyed firing a good-natured barb. "He'd kid anybody," Paterno recalled. "I don't care if the Pope came in, he'd have a little needle. He'd want to know where he got that gown or something."

The trait helped win him friends and influence. A caring and remarkably involved father for the era—Angelo would assume a leadership position on the Brooklyn Prep parents council when his sons attended that prestigious Jesuit high school—he also learned to turn a deaf ear to his opinionated, strong-willed wife.

If Joe Paterno inherited an intellectual, idealistic nature from his father, his competitive, energetic, perfectionist spirit undoubtedly derived from his mother. Florence DeLasalle Cafiero was born on August 21, 1896, one of ten children of energetic Neapolitan immigrants. The Cafieros were the flip side of the Paternos. According to Joe's brother, George, the Cafieros were "fiercely clannish, ferociously competitive, had great street smarts and animal instincts…and boy, were they tough."

Florence was fairer than her husband. She insisted her children work hard, exhibit good manners outside the home, excel in whatever they attempted, and dress immaculately. "We used to joke about her making us wear a shirt and sometimes a tie just to put out the garbage," George said.

In virtually every photo that has survived from their childhoods, the Paterno boys are outfitted in clean white shirts, polished shoes, and pressed trousers or knickers. Even the sneakers they wear in one photo are astonishingly white for such a gritty urban landscape. She would rise before dawn to launder their clothes so that no one would ever have a reason to disparage her boys.

"She was fervent that outsiders not think of us as a family of wops," Joe Paterno would say. "Mom never took a back seat to anyone, any place, any time. If she couldn't be the head of the pack, she wouldn't go."

Her father, who had come to America as a teenager and then returned to Italy to wed, came back to raise his family in the Bedford-Stuyvesant neighborhood of Brooklyn. He delivered peanuts and produce on Long Island, eventually expanding the business sufficiently to replace horses and wagons with trucks.

Growing up in a loud, proud, and opinionated family, Florence developed all of those qualities. She would be the reason her family moved so often, climbing the ladder of Flatbush respectability all the while. "She was driven by the need to be better than everyone," George said.

Curiously, in a nearby Brooklyn neighborhood in the 1920s, another young Italian who also would win glory as a football coach was being raised in much the same fashion. As *Lombardi*, the hit 2010 Broadway play about the Green Bay Packers coaching legend, would make clear, Vince Lombardi's mother, Matty, was no less demanding than Florence Paterno.

In fact, the similarities between Lombardi and Paterno, 13 years younger, are striking. Italians. Brooklynites. Grandsons of barbers. Class presidents in high school. Altar boys. Longtime assistant coaches. And, most significantly, the sons of demanding mothers who initially would be disappointed in their sons' career choices.

During the play, Marie Lombardi, Vince's wife, says with a note of exasperation, "His mother was a perfectionist." Matty Lombardi prayed daily with her son, pushing him in ways that ensured he forever pursued his goals with zeal. She prayed regularly that one of her son's goals would be to become a priest.

The two sides of the parental Paternos' personalities would surface during meals when heated debates on virtually any subject took place. "At the dinner table we were allowed to talk about anything," Paterno once said. "And we did. You name it, we'd argue about it. Kids from the neighborhood would walk into our kitchen, unannounced, and sit in just to listen." It was, Paterno would note, a typical Italian home. "We spoke with flying hands as well as competing voices."

Decades later, when Joe Paterno attended informal Friday night cocktail sessions with the sportswriters who covered his team, the writers would be astounded both by the breadth of subjects Paterno would raise and by the passion of his convictions.

Joe was the oldest of four children. George was 20 months younger. A younger brother named Franklin—an homage to Angelo Paterno's favorite contemporary politician—died in infancy. A sister, Florence, was born in 1937.

Paterno would become, to an extraordinary degree, an amalgam of the best qualities of mother and father. "A superior hybrid offspring," was how George described him. That yin-yang parental influence would both hone and soften the qualities that a Flatbush childhood had implanted in the future coach.

While Paterno understandably has boiled down his childhood to a series of anecdotes—his father's hunger for education, his mother's pride, the influence of Brooklyn Prep's Jesuits, his Gold Dust Twins pairing in Prep's backfield with George—his brother George, who died in 2002, had a much more nuanced view.

A younger brother in the shadows, George recalls his boyhood in much the same way Robert Barone, the put-upon fictional brother from TV's *Everybody Loves Raymond*, might.

"From the time of his birth, Joe was always the top banana in our mother's eyes," George would write, "and would remain that way until she died. Her influence on him was so great she forgave his shortcomings and almost eulogized him, instilling great inner confidence…something the other children lacked."

While Joe willingly adhered to his doting mother's wishes, George chafed. "Joe was her favorite, and she worshipped him.… As I grew up, I resented her attitude and unfairness."

That difference is almost visible in the photos of the two boys. While Joe is invariably poised and smiling, confident in the foreground, George lurks slightly behind, an expression on his face that appears to mix self-doubt and resentment.

While Joe went off to Penn State and fame, it was George who remained home with aging parents. When Angelo died suddenly of a heart attack in 1955, it was George who was there handling matters. While Joe found contentment in a town, a school, and a woman, George flitted from job to job, relationship to relationship, bar to bar.

In George's *The Coach from Byzantium*, a rambling book that was part memoir, part biography of his more famous sibling, and part lament, George wrote of how he differed from the brother he simultaneously loved and was overshadowed by.

"Joe's need to be number one applied not only to sports but also to studies. He was the darling of all of his teachers, the nuns at St. Edmund's, the Jesuits at Brooklyn Prep, and later the professors at Brown. While I hated school, he loved it. While I was content to just get by, he always wanted to be tops in his class.... I am not sure what Dad thought about me, but my mother certainly didn't understand me. Even if I did not realize it, in some ways I was the antithesis of Joe: a free spirit."

In a neighborhood where ethnic and religious differences were sharply defined, where Jews, Italians, Irish, and blacks were disparaged by each other's slurs, there was no way Florence Paterno was going to allow her beloved eldest son to attend public school.

Her boys were enrolled in St. Edmond's parish school in Sheepshead Bay where they were taught by Dominican nuns every bit as tough and demanding as their mother. There they were called "wop" and "dago" by Irish and German classmates, and they returned the favor.

Joe would prove to be an eager and attentive student. "He was all business," George would say. "Joe always was excessively serious and focused. When most of his peers were silly and out looking for fun, his objectives were to be first in everything. My dad was proud, but my mother took it for granted."

Joe Paterno would say he was driven to outperform his classmates because he understood that in doing so he was defending the honor of his family and his heritage. "My mother always said two things—her parents came over here to be

Americans, not Italians, and we never were to forget we were Italians," he said. There is a mid-1930s photo of Joe Paterno that speaks to his focus. The young boy is doing his homework. Wearing knickers, long socks, and a clean white shirt, he is curled up in a sturdy chair, clutching a pen in one hand and a notebook in the other. The image might have come from decades later when as a coach he constantly drew up plays or jotted notes to himself and others. The boy's head is cocked in a pose of understanding, and his determined eyes are focused on the task. For Paterno, schoolwork—all of life, really—was serious business.

Still, there was plenty of time for life beyond the books. Flatbush housed numerous movie theaters, and Paterno could frequently be found in them. Like most young boys, his tastes ran toward epic adventures, particularly those like *The Adventures of Robin Hood* and *Gunga Din*, in which the action was flavored with a Victorian idealism.

Sundays were devoted to family, and with 15 aunts and uncles, there were always dozens of cousins around. "We used to visit and go out together," Paterno said in 1971. "Not like today when you go out with your friends. Our family were our friends."

Residing in relatively tiny dwellings and with little to hold their attention indoors, Brooklyn's Depression-era children spent much of their existence on the sidewalks and streets, playing, fighting, bonding, and courting. The science-fiction writer Isaac Asimov, who grew up in the borough at roughly the same time as Paterno, described what it was like on those crowded blocks. "Night was a wonderful time in Brooklyn in the 1930s. Air conditioning was unknown except in movie houses, and so was television. There was nothing to keep one in the house. Furthermore, few people owned automobiles, so there was nothing to carry one away. That left the streets and the stoops."

Sports were a great passion for the Paterno boys and their crowd of friends. Neighborhood boys played stickball, boxball, and stoopball. Angelo Paterno had played some semipro football for a team in his Bay Ridge neighborhood, and he introduced his sons to the game early. High school football was exceedingly popular then, with the best of those games garnering crowds and newspaper attention rivaling the borough's own NFL team, the Brooklyn Dodgers, who like their baseball namesakes also played in Ebbets Field.

Joe was on St. Edmund's basketball team as a youngster, and he and his Flatbush pals played marathons of basketball and football in nearby Prospect and Marine Parks. "I'd get on the bike, go to Marine Park, get there at 6 or 7 o'clock," Paterno said. "Mom packed me a lunch. I'd be there all day."

St. Edmund's did not offer football, but one of the parish priests started an unofficial team of seventh- and eighth-graders. George said there was never any question about who was in charge during its practices and games. Joe would do the quarterbacking, literally and figuratively.

Joe and George followed their athletic heroes closely in the sports sections of the *Brooklyn Eagle* and the many New York dailies. Though until 1941 the baseball Dodgers were mediocre at best, Paterno attended their games whenever possible. In the summer of 1943, in fact, two years after Leo Durocher's pennant-winners had re-ignited the borough's baseball passions, the 16-year-old Paterno would work as an Ebbets Field usher.

Sometimes Paterno and his pals would hop on the subway to Manhattan and go to basketball games at old Madison Square Garden, then the capital of the college game. They'd buy hot-beef sandwiches at a nearby storefront and then sit in the old arena's dark upper reaches, dreaming of themselves competing against the players they saw far below, players like Hank Luisetti or George Mikan, the 6'10" bespectacled DePaul All-American whom Paterno said "looked like a freak."

He listened to baseball on the radio, too, as well as to broadcasts of Joe Louis' fights and big college football games, particularly those of the patron team of most young Depression-era Catholic boys, Notre Dame. As for pro football, the New York Giants were his favorites, an allegiance he would mention much later when he was offered the chance to coach them.

It was while Joe, George, and Angelo were listening to a Dodgers football game on the radio in the parlor of their 23rd Street apartment, that they learned about the bombing of Pearl Harbor.

By then, Paterno was attending Brooklyn Prep.

3

FOUNDED IN 1908 BY THE JESUITS, Brooklyn Prep was located on Carroll Street, a 40-minute bus ride away from the Paternos' Flatbush residence.

A Jesuit education in the 1940s was not for the faint of heart. As is stressed in literature from that most intellectual of all Catholic orders, in words that might have been cribbed from a Penn State football brochure, a Jesuit education is "a call to human excellence, to the fullest possible development of all human qualities. It is a call to critical thinking and disciplined studies, a call to develop the whole person, head and heart, intellect and feelings."

It developed young men through a reliance on classical tools—particularly Latin and Greek—and a discipline that included strict codes of dress and behavior. All of that was welcomed by the teenaged Paterno, who would hone his instinct for order there and carry it into his coaching career.

Brooklyn Prep had about 800 male students when Angelo Paterno made his first tuition payment. Joe had qualified for scholarships to a few other Catholic high schools, but not surprisingly, Joe was insistent on challenging himself at the Prep. Its $210 annual tuition was a bit steep for the family, especially when George followed him there a year later, but both father and son recognized what a good fit the school was.

"The Jesuit influence was the perfect catalyst to hone his innate strengths and temper the explosive personality with calculating patience and manipulative skills," George wrote.

As a freshman, the 14-year-old Joe threw himself into school in the classroom and beyond. Even though the student population was primarily Irish, he would be elected a class officer in each of his four years there, vice president as a junior and president as a senior. He also joined the Book Discussion and Sodality Clubs and became a leader on the Prep's mediocre basketball team.

"[Paterno] really knew more about the game than the coach," basketball teammate Walter McCurdy told Paterno biographer Michael O'Brien. "He was pretty much running the team. He was a natural-born leader."

But weighing just 125 pounds as a freshman, Paterno did not try out for the football team. He did in his sophomore year, by which time Brooklyn Prep had a new coach.

Earl "Zev" Graham, a native of Akron, Ohio, had been Fordham's star quarterback in the 1920s. His nickname was a reference to an outstanding racehorse of the period. Graham kept the skinny sophomore on the squad, though he was used as an occasional kick-returner and special-teams player and not as the guard Paterno had hoped to be.

The following year, however, when Paterno had fleshed out his 5'10" frame, Graham gave the feisty junior a shot at guard. He did little there to distinguish himself. It wouldn't be until he was a senior that Paterno found his football niche.

Early in that 1944 season, Graham, impressed by the youngster's constant questioning and his understanding of the game, made Paterno his quarterback. The coach had installed a no-huddle offense, and he needed someone who could think on his feet to run it. The skinny senior loved the position's leadership responsibilities and mental challenges. "He just took over," wrote George, who was a star Prep running back by then. "If he could not beat you physically, he would try to outthink you."

Though quarterbacks in Graham's offense rarely threw the ball, Paterno was worried about his arm strength. A natural left-hander who passed right-handed because his first baseball glove had been for righties, he would term his throwing style "a shot-put." He would fire a football against a basement wall for hours at a time to try to improve. "The fear of deficiency made me push myself to the limit," Paterno said. "If you let them, the fear of weaknesses and adversities can whip you down. But they can also whip you up. And between those choices, I already instinctively sensed, every person has the power to choose."

The team responded to his leadership and to his play, along with that of brother George, a running back. "[Joe] wasn't fast," said Bill Conlin, a future Philadelphia sportswriter who grew up in Brooklyn and later covered the man he had watched play high school football, "but he was an amazingly elusive broken-field runner who looked like his hips were on ball bearings."

The school's newspaper called Joe Paterno "the brains of the team." The Prep became one of the city's top scholastic teams, going 6–1–1 and outscoring opponents by a margin of 197–52 that season. Its only defeat came on November 5, 1944, a 20–13 loss to St. Cecilia's from Englewood, New Jersey, before a crowd of 10,000. St. Cecilia's was coached by Vince Lombardi.

Joe had hurt his shoulder before that game and, without acknowledging it, played in pain throughout. "Considering that Joe Paterno's shoulder made him useless as a runner and a defenseman, I'd say we were lucky to keep it close," Graham said afterward.

If Joe was the leader, George was the team's best runner. One sportswriter in that nickname-happy era of sports journalism even dubbed the brothers the "Gold Dust Twins." By even his brother's admission, George was the better athlete. But their mother, fearing her younger son might eclipse the beloved first-born, counseled George to restrain himself for his brother's sake. If he did so, the strategy worked. Joe was named to the *New York World-Telegram*'s All-Metropolitan team that year.

Paterno likes to say he was a better basketball player. A guard, he played three years on a varsity team that never achieved a .500 record. He was the team's captain as a senior.

Meanwhile, having received his law degree in 1941 and working courtroom hours, Angelo was able to attend most of his sons' games. So regular a presence was Angelo at the school's athletic events that when Brooklyn Prep scheduled its first all-sports banquet in 1945, he was made the co-chairman.

During high school summers, Joe Paterno worked as a Penn Station baggage checker, a mail clerk at a summer camp in the Catskills, and as an Ebbets Field usher. The baseball duty came during a season when the World War II–depleted Dodgers finished in seventh place, 28 games below .500 and 42 games behind the first-place Cardinals. Since the Dodgers drew just 605,905 fans that summer—a little less than 8,000 a game—there couldn't have been too much ushering to do or too many tips to reward his efforts.

Just as his senior year of high school would launch Paterno toward a career in football, it also solidified his thinking. He would graduate from Brooklyn Prep certain he was headed for greatness. The men responsible for implanting that sense of destiny in an already idealistic teenager were the long-dead Roman poet Virgil and a 25-year-old Jesuit apprentice named Thomas Bermingham.

Bermingham, Paterno's Latin instructor in the fall of 1944, would become a favorite of the boy and a lifelong friend. When Bermingham learned that the youngster had an interest in serious literature—Paterno had listed Fitzgerald, Hemingway, and Steinbeck as favorite authors on a school survey—he asked the student if he'd like to meet after school three times a week to read Virgil's *The Aeneid* in its original Latin. Ever the earnest student and always ready for a challenge, Paterno jumped at the opportunity.

"I had a sense that this young man had read far beyond his years and was still reading on his own," Bermingham said. "I called him after class and I said, 'Joseph, I can't make you but I would love to have you do much more than the rest of the class.' And, typical Joe Paterno, he jumped at that chance."

The opening line of *The Aeneid*—*Arma virumque cano, Troiae qui primus ab oris*, or, "Of arms and the man I sing"—struck an immediate chord with the impressionable student. "It made me hear cymbals and trumpets.... I still feel the spell of that young robed cleric's eyes searing into me, reminding me that I was special and that this was important," he said later

The story, written between 29 and 19 B.C., was as compelling for Paterno as any Errol Flynn movie adventure. "He endures battles, storms, shipwrecks, and the rages of the gods," Paterno wrote of Aeneas. "But the worst storm is the one that rages within himself. He yearns to be free of his tormenting duty, but he knows that his duty is to others, to his men. Through years of hardship and peril, Aeneas reluctantly but relentlessly heeds his [fate] until he founds Rome." Aeneas recognized and honored his destiny as a leader, and he could not and would not be swayed from meeting it. Neither would Paterno.

"I don't think anybody can get a handle on what makes me tick as a person," Paterno wrote in his autobiography, "and certainly can't get at the roots of how I coach football without understanding what I learned from the deep relationship I formed with Virgil during those afternoons and later in my life…. Once a person has experienced a genuine masterpiece, the size and scope of it last as a memory forever."

Aeneas' journey would provide many of the lessons Paterno looked to when he became a coach. "Aeneas is not a grandstanding superstar," Paterno wrote. "Aeneas cannot choose not to found Rome. He's destined to create it. But he has to struggle with himself, inch by inch, hour by hour—play by play—to figure out how to do it, to endure the struggle and torment of doing it, and take all the bad breaks along the way." One can almost hear Paterno following that up with, "Now get out there and kick Ohio State's butt!"

Bermingham, who was at the beginning of the lengthy journey necessary to become a Jesuit, would have a similar impact on another Brooklyn Prep student, William Blatty. The priest would go on to write the best-seller *The Exorcist*. Bermingham would have a small role in the movie version as Georgetown's president and would be the film's spiritual adviser.

• • •

In February 1945—war demands had altered the typical school year—Paterno, the salutatorian in a class of '42, graduated from Brooklyn Prep in a ceremony held at the larger Bishop McDonnell High School.

Paterno's senior photo portrays a confident adolescent. Among the activities listed below the picture are student council, student government, book club, a religious organization, and several sports.

While awaiting a draft notice, Paterno took a job at Brooklyn Prep, assisting the school's athletic director, Rev. Francis Brock. And ironically for someone who would spend decades railing against the evil influences of boosters, Paterno was reeled in by one of that breed.

Sometime that spring, Zev Graham showed up at the Paternos' home with a proposition. The high school coach had a friend named Everett "Busy" Arnold, a successful comic book publisher in Manhattan and a Brown University alum. Graham told the youngster's father that Arnold was recruiting football talent for his alma mater, and he had seen the boy's name listed on the All-Metropolitan team. If the youngster played for Brown, Arnold would take care of all of Paterno's expenses, a practice not yet outlawed by the NCAA.

"I used to get a check from a foundation that Mr. Arnold had set up, and I would take it down to the bursar's office," Paterno said. "He must have been taking care of about 18 or 20 players, and we all appreciated his help. But that's all we got—just the money for our tuition, room and board, and books. Not another cent."

Paterno visited the school in Providence, Rhode Island, met the football coach, a pleasant silver-haired man named Charles "Rip" Engle, and was impressed. The war had not yet ended, but Paterno, an 18-year-old draft-eligible male, decided to enroll at Brown that June. Six weeks later, by which time the war in Europe already had ended, his draft notice came through.

He did his basic training at Fort Dix in New Jersey and was there on V-J Day. He would be sent to Korea, where he served as a radio operator, and in late August 1946 he was discharged from the army. Paterno would never talk much about his brief and unremarkable military service other than to point out how glad he was to resume his studies at Brown.

Founded in 1763 when the Philadelphia Association of Baptist Churches dispatched Rev. James Manning to Providence to form a college there, Brown was by 1946 an elite institution favored by those wealthy New England scions who, for whatever reason, didn't go to Yale or Harvard. It was not yet officially Ivy League; that affiliation of eight private Eastern colleges wouldn't come into existence until 1954.

Paterno would always appreciate his Brown education and even more so as the years passed. But the passage for an Italian Catholic from Brooklyn's streets into New England's WASPy society was not an easy one. Ultimately, the truest reflection of how Paterno felt about his undergraduate experience might be found in his 1989 autobiography, in the title he gave the chapter that dealt with it: "Not-So-Divine Providence."

A practical uncle had recommended Paterno major in engineering, but the freshman student quickly found the subject matter "boring" and switched to English literature. "[I] never regretted it for a moment," he said. "The Romantic period held my interest most. I'm a romantic. I dreamed then, and do now, about gladiators and knights winning battles. I like the movie *Patton*. George Patton, a high-minded lover of poetry and epics, believed he was reincarnated, probably from a previous life as a Roman general. My kind of guy."

As it turned out, Paterno would need Patton's toughness to deal with some of the slights he experienced at Brown. Invited to a fraternity party his freshman year, Paterno showed up in a white sweater. "I walked into a calm sea of blue blazers, sharkskin suits, and Harris tweeds. I knew I had blown something when all those cool-eyed faces turned toward me and my sweater, slowly, so as not to tip and spill their stemmed glasses that seemed to hold nothing but clear water, except for an olive in each. I heard somebody whisper, 'How did that Dago get invited?' They never asked me back."

Years later Paterno would say he still could sense those people "studying me out of the corners of their eyes." He felt the same kind of condescending attitude in class but unwilling to confirm his classmates' skewed perceptions, it motivated him to work harder. Before long, he was excelling in his academic work and not only was admitted to a fraternity, Delta Kappa Epsilon, but he also became the chapter's vice president.

His progress was slow and steady on the football field, too. Engle and his assistant, Weeb Ewbank, liked the brainy youngster immediately. They installed him at safety where he gained a reputation as a ball hawk and a hard tackler.

He added punt- and kick-returner to his resume as a junior, totaling 146 yards of returns in an upset of Princeton. That same year, Engle began experimenting with him at quarterback, and by his senior year the position was Paterno's. George, also the beneficiary of Arnold's generosity, again teamed up with his older brother in the backfield.

Paterno grasped Engle's Wing-T offense better than anyone. And that understanding more than his physical talents would help lead Brown to an 8–1 record his senior season; their only defeat came at Princeton. New York sportswriter Stanley Woodward would presciently say of Brown's quarterback, "He can't run, and he can't pass. All he can do is think—and win."

On defense in that one-platoon era, Paterno, a co-captain along with Joe Scott, had six interceptions, giving him a school-record 14 for his career.

"Joe was a great student, an excellent athlete, and a popular leader," said Scott, who went on to become the CEO of Vicks.

That season, Paterno had given up basketball, a sport he'd played in his first three years at Brown, perhaps because he'd measured himself against future NBA Hall of Famer Bob Cousy in a loss to Holy Cross and decided football better served his talents.

Engle's relationship with his quarterback grew so close that in the spring of 1950, the coach asked Paterno to help train his successor at quarterback during spring practice. The eager and eternal student prepared by reading guides on coaching and books famous quarterbacks had written. He was enjoying himself in this new role when a rumor began to circulate that Engle had interviewed for the head coaching job at Penn State.

4

Good speed to your youthful valor, boy!
So shall you scale the stars.

—Virgil, *The Aeneid*

A 23-year-old New Yorker whose ambition would be shaped more by his fascination with the mythical journey of Aeneas than by the real dreams of his immigrant Italian parents, Paterno began a life-altering expedition of his own in May 1950.

Years earlier, he had found in *The Aeneid*'s courageous Trojan hero his life's model. "Destiny has struck him with being a leader, and he can't escape it," Paterno said of Aeneas. That belief, that vision of himself as a fated moral warrior, a man with a mission, would explain much about the rest of Paterno's life, including why he and Rip Engle were departing Providence, Rhode Island, that late-spring morning and heading for State College in Pennsylvania.

In the midst of America's post–World War II optimism, virtually anything seemed possible. In that spirit, these two men, Brown University's coach and senior quarterback the previous football season, were making the 342-mile journey to Penn State.

State College was a tiny green bullseye near the exact center of Pennsylvania, a conservative valley village of 23,000 people. In the decades to come, much as Aeneas had done in founding Rome, Paterno would help create a shining community there. Through the force of his will, he would construct a Penn State myth and in the process transform "Happy Valley" into the center of an empire. But that was all in the misty future. That May morning, he was merely a fidgety, somewhat reluctant passenger in Engle's Cadillac heading for a white-bread town where, as he later lamented, "they put celery in the spaghetti sauce."

These two traveling companions were each exemplars of their disparate hometowns. Engle—prematurely silver-haired at 44 with tan skin, blue eyes that sparkled, and a gentle spirit—was the epitome of distinguished. "Throw a black robe over his shoulders," a later *Sports Illustrated* profile would note, "and he could play the part of a Supreme Court justice." But there were dark worry rings beneath those eyes, and he was inclined to see any glass as half-full.

A one-time mule driver from Elk Lick, Pennsylvania, Engle was reserved by nature, and some would call him glum. "Rip's not happy unless he's sad," said Syracuse's coach Ben Schwartzwalder, one of his great rivals. A *Providence Journal* columnist once wrote, "Rip has never been known for his optimism.… In a profession noted for its weepers, [he] is in a class by himself."

Paterno, meanwhile, was Brooklyn-born, dark-haired, swarthy, restless, talkative, cocky, optimistic—and, as the rest of Engle's staff would soon learn, opinionated. "I was a such a damn loudmouth," Paterno wrote of his younger self. "I couldn't keep quiet when I thought things weren't going right." Not surprisingly, while the younger man deferred to his mentor in most matters, he did most of the talking on the trip.

As with any significant historical figure, it's interesting to ponder the tiny moments, the casual decisions and unexpected encounters that come together to form a noteworthy career. There would be numerous occasions when Paterno could easily have veered off the road he now says destiny set him upon. Though most would come at the start of his journey, there would be potential missteps and detours for decades, points at which a single hurried choice, one fit of spite, or a particularly enticing whiff of wealth and fame could have waylaid him. If not for what seems, in retrospect, a fortuitous chain of events, he might have turned away from or never even reached Penn State. He could just as easily have headed for law school or later the NFL, Yale, or Southern California. Instead, against all odds, he came to State College and stayed for a lifetime. And it is that staying as much as the astounding longevity that sets apart Paterno's career.

None of it would have happened without Engle. His was the star Paterno followed. If Engle had stayed at Brown, if he had not been so enamored of the Wing-T and his young quarterback, if he had not been a native Pennsylvanian, if he had been given more than one hire at Penn State, if he had been able to convince a single veteran assistant to join him in State College, Paterno today almost certainly would be a retired New England lawyer.

• • •

Charles Albert "Rip" Engle may have resembled a patrician, but his background was covered with dirt and coal dust. Born on March 20, 1906, in Elk Lick, a tiny south-central Pennsylvania mining community that was a universe removed from Brooklyn, Engle apparently earned his distinctive nickname when as a rough-and-tumble schoolboy he tore the same pair of pants four times in a single week.

Curiously for a man who would letter in four sports in college and go on to a career as a football coach, Engle did not play any sports at Salisbury High School. He was too busy.

Though his father allegedly promised each of his six children $100 if they reached the age of 21 without having tried tobacco or alcohol, the Quaker family struggled financially. To help, Engle went to work at 14, driving mule teams in the coal mines. "I learned how to work hard from those mules," he would say. A natural and easygoing leader, Engle was a foreman by 19. Eventually, he saved enough money to enroll at Blue Ridge College, a now-defunct school in New Windsor, Maryland.

Blue Ridge played football, but just barely. In 1927, with Engle an inexperienced end, it would lose to Temple 110–0 and finish a winless season without having scored a point. The football and social life at nearby Western Maryland College in Westminster seemed considerably more promising, and after a year Engle transferred there. It was at Western Maryland, now McDaniel College, where he found a wife, Mary Weber "Sunny" Broughton, and a deeper interest in organized sports.

He would play baseball, basketball, tennis, and football there, but it was the last that captured his imagination. A chemistry major, Engle liked football's X-and-O volatility and its tactical challenges. He enjoyed outthinking, outworking, and particularly outfoxing opponents. He and Coach Dick Harlow, a former star and coach at Penn State, developed a strong bond.

Football's demand for discipline fit Engle's personality perfectly. He was a meticulous man who dressed neatly, liked good cars, rarely swore, and did not drink or smoke. Above all, he had a Pennsylvania German's admiration for order. He understood very early that football was played best where there was a well-defined structure to practices, games, and the lives and professional duties of players and coaches.

After graduation, Engle taught mathematics and coached basketball at Waynesboro High School, 80 miles east of Elk Lick. Like Paterno two decades later, Engle would live with an older couple, in this case school board president Charles Speck and his wife, until he married in the summer of 1931. When Waynesboro football's coach, P.E. Probst, retired, Engle succeeded him. The 24-year-old, whose wavy hair already was graying, would be tremendously successful. In 11 years, his Waynesboro teams would capture eight conference titles.

In the meantime, Charlie Havens, a former Western Maryland classmate, had succeeded Harlow at their alma mater. Havens asked Engle to be his assistant and he agreed, coaching the varsity ends and the freshman team, which went 4–0–1 in his first season. His reputation was growing, at least among the fraternity of men who had played or coached at Western Maryland.

In 1942, while working on a master's degree in education, he was contacted by another college head coach with a Western Maryland connection, Brown University's Neil "Skip" Stahley. A Penn State graduate, Stahley had been a Western Maryland assistant and he too was impressed by Engle...so much so that he hired him as Brown's offensive line coach.

Brown's greatest football days were by then behind them. Fritz Pollard, the first black All-American, had starred at the school on a Providence hillside. He was a running back in 1916 when Brown became the first team to beat Harvard and Yale in the same season, earning a Rose Bowl bid. (Washington State won 14–0.) In 1926, Coach Tuss McLaughry's team famously went two consecutive games—victories over Yale and Dartmouth—without a single substitution. Six years later, Brown managed to defeat seven consecutive unbeaten opponents. Stahley was hired in 1941 and would compile a 14–11 record in three seasons there.

When Stahley enlisted in the Navy after the 1943 season, Engle, who by then had a nine-year-old son and a deferment, replaced him. His first three Bruins teams finished with records less than .500. In 1946, he got his first look at Paterno. And with the New Yorker playing a key role on both sides of the ball as a junior and especially a senior, Engle's last two Brown squads would go a combined 15–3 in 1948 and 1949.

By that time the GI Bill, which provided federal funds for millions of returning veterans seeking an education, was transforming every aspect of American college life. It greatly increased student populations, which precipitated campus building booms everywhere. At Penn State, for example, enrollment swelled from 6,000 in 1938 to a record 10,200 in 1946, and 55 percent were veterans. A year later, the surge continued and the percentage of veterans jumped to 80 percent. That necessitated new housing. Makeshift living quarters for veterans and their families—called veterans villages—were hastily constructed on the east end of campus.

Competing now for a wave of new students and for more plentiful federal research dollars, Penn State and other schools saw sports as a way to enhance their brand and generate both revenue and applications. Colleges constructed new athletic facilities or upgraded old ones. As a result, the best coaches suddenly found themselves in great demand, a trend that created a coaching carousel. Eventually it stopped for Engle.

Content at Brown, especially after the 1948–49 successes, Engle received a call from Pitt athletic director Tom Hamilton in the spring of 1950. There, Coach Mike Milligan had resigned and the Panthers, who were in the midst of an unsuccessful effort to replace the University of Chicago as a Big Ten member, needed a successor. Engle interviewed, but it remains unclear whether he turned Pitt down or if the reverse was true. In any event, Len Casanova, who was out of job after Santa Clara dropped football earlier that year, was hired. Casanova lasted just one season before Hamilton himself took over.

Penn State was among the many schools making a coaching change in 1950, and not long after Engle's Pitt flirtation, he got a call from Nittany Lions athletic director Carl Schott. The administrator wasn't taking a shot in the dark. Engle was a well-known commodity in State College. His uncle, Lloyd Engle, had been a tackle at Penn State from 1910–12. One of Lloyd Engle's Nittany Lions teammates had been Harlow, who before mentoring Rip at Western Maryland had been Penn State's head coach.

Harlow, pointing to Engle's record at Waynesboro and Brown, strongly recommended his former player to both Schott and powerful athletic board member Dutch Herman. In mid-April, Engle traveled to State College to meet with Schott and interim president James Milholland. Soon afterward he was offered and accepted the position.

In addition to his personal Penn State connections, there were several good reasons for Engle's decision. First, the new job would bring him closer to his aging parents, who lived in nearby Somerset County. Second, after years of meandering from school to school, he could gain some security by earning tenure as a full professor in the athletic department. Third, Pennsylvania was teeming with high school football talent. And finally, and maybe most significantly, Penn State, after a long hiatus, was recommitting to football in a big way by reinstituting athletic scholarships and refurbishing and expanding Beaver Field.

Schott and Engle agreed to keep the news secret while the coach went through the formality of asking Brown for permission to talk with Penn State. But somehow, even before Engle had departed State College for home, word got out, hastening the transition process.

One of Schott's hiring stipulations was that Engle retain all of Penn State's assistants. Engle, knowing he wanted to install the more complicated Wing-T offense at a place that had been running the Single Wing since practically the turn of the century, convinced Schott to allow him to bring along one new aide. That's when the dominoes began to tumble Paterno's way.

In hiring that new assistant, Engle might have asked Ewbank, but the Brown assistant had agreed to rejoin his old navy buddy, Paul Brown, on the staff of the NFL's Browns. Engle might have asked assistant Bob Priestley, but Priestley had accepted the head job at Norwich College. He did ask assistant Gus Zitrides, but Zitrides would stay to become Brown's next head coach. He also asked assistant Bill Doolittle, but Doolittle preferred to remain at Brown with Zitrides.

Finally, there was only one other available person who knew the offense well enough to teach it—his graduating quarterback. Lured by the prospect of adventure, a meaningful odyssey of his own, Joe Paterno agreed to go along. "He was very intelligent," Engle said, "and crazy about football."

• • •

Engle was crazy about cars and driving. The more challenging the terrain and weather conditions, the more he enjoyed motoring through them. Even in the spring, the curvy mountain roads and steep inclines that led to Happy Valley could make for nerve-wracking journeys. Not for Engle. For him, there were few things as relaxing as driving up and down hills, surrounded by the natural beauty of central Pennsylvania, and all the better if snow and ice were added to the mix. Trying to fill the 50 new scholarships, Engle would drive 30,000 miles his first year at Penn State, much of it in winter. A friend was so impressed that he gave Engle a sign for his car's visor that read, "Rip Engle: World Famous Snow, Ice and Fog Driver."

The weather was tranquil that May as Engle and Paterno entered Pennsylvania. The two men carried on a steady conversation about a variety of subjects. Football was prominent, of course, and they talked of their plans for practice routines and coaching responsibilities, as well as what they could do better and differently at Penn State. Along the way, Engle also gave the New Yorker an idea of what he could expect in central Pennsylvania. "I remember he told me everything was so clean," Paterno recalled. "He said you could eat off the floors of the barns."

But the nearer they got to their destination, the more subdued Paterno became. As the landscape turned increasingly pastoral—the spare farms and stone barns reminiscent of the stark, moody paintings of native son Andrew Wyeth—he seemed to be questioning his decision more deeply. The unease was understandable.

Paterno had recently finished his senior year at Brown, earning a degree in English literature. He had passed the law boards easily and had been accepted for the fall semester at Boston University's law school. That was gratifying news for his parents. His father had loaned him $2,000 to get started at BU.

A lawyer himself, Angelo Paterno had endured years of night-school classes to achieve his dream at age 44. His mother had always pushed her oldest son to achieve and excel. In Paterno's mind, he could hear her crowing proudly, "My son, the lawyer."

But the dutiful son unexpectedly disappointed them when a few weeks before Brown's June 9 commencement, he told his parents he was putting his law education on hold to follow Engle. Never impulsive, Paterno appeared to have given little thought to what would be the single most significant decision of his life. He thought it might be fun for a year, and if things didn't work out, the money he earned would help him pay back his father.

Paterno's mother did not understand. His father was puzzled, too, but he was more supportive. Perhaps because his own quixotic accomplishment was still fresh in his mind, Angelo Paterno at least offered his son, who would be paid $3,600 a year, some comforting counsel. "I never made any real money," he told him, "but I'm doing what I want to do. That's more important than money. If you like coaching, then stay with it."

Would Paterno like coaching? He couldn't have known the answer then. His only experience had come in the past few weeks, when he'd helped out at Brown's spring practices. Still, the possibility itched.

He had always been curious, and he'd always enjoyed captaining, directing, and leading. That didactic streak, which was not always his most endearing quality, would never go away. Even into his eighties, Paterno could not resist an impulse to coach, whether it was nudging sportswriters toward a particular story line; counseling his players on fashion, grooming, and football; or offering advice to assistants. His whiningly persistent instructions were the soundtrack of Penn State football. Departed players would swear they could hear that voice in their heads for years afterward. Most had refined personalized imitations of their coach's squeaky carping. "Geez, Wisniewski, we're gonna get licked on Saturday if that's the best you can do!" That thin Brooklyn-accented voice might have brought to mind bad World War II movies or hack comedians, but if it was directed at you, it took on considerable heft. "If you're on the receiving end," said Charlie Pittman, a star running back for one of Paterno's early teams, "he sounds like James Earl Jones."

Soon the two travelers had passed Harrisburg, the capital of the state that in 1950 was still the nation's third most populous. (Pennsylvania's 10.5 million residents were only 150,000 fewer than No. 2 California's total.) And the state was still flush with railroad, coal, and steel riches. Curiously, that wealth had not funneled into the Pennsylvania State College, the commonwealth's lightly-regarded land-grant school.

Tuition there in 1950 was $200, even though the cost of educating each student was $600. The gap was bridged by a compliant legislature, many of whom began attending Penn State football games—free of charge, of course. While many on the state's more urban edges called the college where agricultural studies had long dominated "Farmers U," postwar demographics were beginning to reshape Penn State. In 1949, its enrollment had reached 13,000. For a first time, it was attracting professors and administrators from beyond Pennsylvania.

Milton Eisenhower, the brother of the World War II hero and future U.S. president, became Penn State's president in July 1950, just three months after Paterno's arrival. By 1953, the school would achieve university status. But in terms of wealth, it remained a decidedly minor-league institution. Its endowment was pitiful, and total contributions—including donations to athletics—had amounted to just $71,000 in 1949.

Eric Walker, who succeeded Eisenhower, would say that financially Penn State's situation was "the worst of two worlds." Because it was not strictly a state school but "state-related," it got far less funding from the legislature than Big Ten schools, and it didn't have a wealthy alumni base like the more prestigious private Eastern schools—the future Ivy League members and even such smaller Pennsylvania colleges as Swarthmore, Lehigh, and Carnegie-Mellon.

President Eisenhower's politically well-connected younger brother wanted to transform Penn State into a nationally recognized university, like those large state schools in the Big Ten, a view that would soon be adopted by Paterno.

Like many in that generation of college leaders, Milton Eisenhower believed football could play a big role in that transformation. Famed scientist Vannevar Bush once told Eisenhower's successor, Walker, "There are three ways to build a great university. You can build a lot of buildings. You can build a football team. Or you can build a great faculty."

While Eisenhower supported all three concepts, he also felt the institution and not the boosters should hold the football reins and hold them tightly. He and the new athletic director he would hire from the University of Michigan, Ernie McCoy, would attempt to impose a moral component on Penn State sports. Athletes would be students first. They should graduate. They should receive no special treatment. Alumni were welcome observers but not participants.

Whether the tone of rectitude they tried to strike was hopelessly naïve or not, it appealed to Paterno, who would work the rest of his life to sell and enhance that image of Penn State sports.

In keeping with that philosophy, it was determined that the newly restored scholarships would be administered by an agency outside of athletics—the Senate Committee on Scholarships and Awards. Athletes were required to meet the same admission standards and follow the same rules of academic progress as other students.

Engle initially balked at the restrictions, pointing out that other football powers—and that clearly is what Penn State was aspiring to be—made frequent academic concessions. McCoy, who arrived in 1952, wouldn't budge. Engle eventually yielded to the administration's guidelines. Paterno and other recruiters were instructed that when they identified a prospect, they should check first with the high school's guidance counselor. If the player's grades were good enough, they could then talk to them. It was not the most effective way to build a college football power in the 1950s. Even McCoy had to acknowledge, "Penn State lost a lot of kids that way."

• • •

Engle's car turned north on Route 322, a two-lane road that paralleled the Susquehanna River before crossing it and winding into the handsome Appalachian Mountains for the final 90 miles to State College. The rural scenery changed to a near-wilderness setting, rolling foothills whose thick blankets of green were punctuated only by an occasional dairy farm.

For a young man whose life had been spent in Brooklyn and Providence, who fancied himself even then as urbane, this might as well have been darkest Africa. The alien landscape only intensified Paterno's doubts. What was he doing here? How could he have walked away from law school for this? He'd never survive out here. He'd help Engle for the summer, perhaps stay for the fall's schedule, and then it was on to Boston.

At Penn State, the third session of spring practice was set to begin that Monday. Assistant Earl Bruce had been running the drills while Engle returned to Providence to attend to some personal business and pick up Paterno. For the first of thousands of times in the next 60 years, Penn State's *Daily Collegian* that Saturday would carry the name Paterno in a headline.

"Paterno, Brown Grid Star, Added to Football Staff," read the three-column headline on page three of the student publication. The story talked mostly about Paterno's play as Brown's quarterback. But Barney Madden, a *Providence Journal* sportswriter, predicted to the article's anonymous author, "You'll like Paterno."

The accompanying photo showed the newest assistant in his Brown uniform, the intensity in his black eyes nearly burning through the page. With no glasses and a thick head of wavy black hair, Paterno resembled the photo of actor Zachary Scott that graced the large ad for Chesterfield cigarettes on an adjacent page.

Finally, sometime late on the afternoon of May 27, 1950, Engle's car pulled into State College. If Paterno had picked up a copy of the student-run newspaper that bore his photo, he'd have gotten a good glimpse of the town he would soon be inhabiting. The movies were closed on Sundays. If he wanted liquor, he couldn't buy it there. And the college that was employing him not only had a Poultry Club, but that group's annual picnic was big enough news to warrant a prominent spot on page two.

5

THE PROGRAM PATERNO WAS STEPPING INTO might not
have been Notre Dame or Army, but it had both history and
promise, although Engle's inherent pessimism seemed to prevent
him from realizing the latter.

The new head coach's standard written response to the many
telegrams and letters of congratulation he received after his April
hiring—to everyone from University of Pennsylvania coach
George Munger to the Cleveland Browns' Paul Brown—included
this phrase: "We are going to have a lot of cloudy days before
the sun shines through."

He needn't have worried. In 1950, the sun still shone brightly
on Pennsylvania, which was rich in the hard-nosed sons of blue-
collar miners and steelworkers. Along with neighboring Ohio,
the Keystone State was widely considered to be the nation's
top producer of football players. On the day his hiring was
announced, Engle alluded to that. "There's plenty of football
talent in this state, and I'm going to go after it," he said. "In the
last 10 years Pennsylvania has turned out more All-Americans
than any other state in the country." The difficulty was convincing
them to stay in-state and, for Penn State, to get them to travel
to faraway State College.

Though the Nittany Lions had plenty of football achievements, they had never been consensus national champions. No Pennsylvania team, despite the All-Americans and professional stars produced there, had won such a title in the last 13 years—not since Pitt in 1937. At the high school level, though, particularly in central and western Pennsylvania and in the coal regions of the northeast, the sport remained as sturdy and strong as the steel the industrial state churned out. Pennsylvanians were crazy about football.

A hybrid of soccer and rugby, by way of Canada, the game that would become American football had taken root at the elite Eastern colleges and in typical U.S. fashion had spread westward. Though a pair of New Jersey schools, Rutgers and Princeton, had participated in the first collegiate game in 1869, it wasn't until 1875 that a contest resembling the modern version of the sport was played.

By the 1880s, a group of Penn State students had formed a football club. On November 5, 1887, that club played its first game, drubbing a squad from nearby Bucknell 54–0. Like the college itself, the sport grew slowly but steadily in the next decade. By 1892 it was established enough to warrant the hiring of a coach, George Hoskins. A year later, a 500-seat wooden grandstand was constructed to accommodate the crowds that had begun gathering for games, which were then played on a lawn in front of Old Main.

Football, by the turn of the century, was firmly established as a favorite extracurricular activity. The student newspaper, then called *The Free Lance*, reported on the contests, and students already were creating such related rituals as organized cheers and fight songs. The band played at the games, and the school's future mascot, the Nittany Lion, would debut in 1906.

A student, Joe Mason, had traveled to Princeton that year for a baseball game and left impressed by the home team's Tiger mascot. Returning to campus, Mason wrote to *The Lemon*, a student publication, urging Penn State to adopt one, too. He suggested a lion, since mountain lions had roamed the surrounding hills as recently as the 1880s. The lion was soon chosen in a student vote, and the area's most prominent peak, Mount Nittany, lent it a first name.

Talk of reform, which would become a Paterno mantra, always hovered close to Penn State football, perhaps because the rugged game stood in such contrast to the state's pacifist Quaker roots. After the onfield deaths of dozens of players nationwide in the early 1900s, the sport was derided by American reformers and academics as too brutal and violent, an activity unworthy of the "gentleman amateur" ideals supposed to govern collegiate athletics. But thanks to rules changes aimed at player safety and the careful shepherding of president Theodore Roosevelt, football survived the national outcry. What wasn't addressed as effectively, however, was the issue of professionalism.

Stories about "tramp athletes"—players with little or no academic credentials being lured to college teams with various incentives, including cash—were widespread in the first decades of the 20th century. Not only did some of these players frequently move from school to school, often for a better offer, some actually withdrew after football season and went elsewhere. That had happened at Penn State. In October 1902, Andrew Smith went from there to the University of Pennsylvania in Philadelphia. Smith had played for the Nittany Lions in a 17–0 loss at Pennsylvania. He apparently played well enough to impress his opponents, however, because two days later he was practicing with Pennsylvania in Philadelphia. He performed in three more games for Penn State before officially transferring to Penn. Smith would earn All-American status at Penn in 1904, then he would drop out of school.

Expanding interest in football among students and alumni and the benefits colleges derived from increased newspaper coverage of the sport led to further growth and abuses. Players, coaches, and sometimes entire teams were being funded through a variety of shady methods, and the enterprises were often run by overzealous alumni. Penn State certainly wasn't immune to the problems.

In spite of the antipathy of faculty and many administrators, trustees there had authorized athletic scholarships as early as 1900, making Penn State one of the first schools to do so. With alumni essentially making the rules, tutoring services were made available to athletes but not the average student. Athletes were housed in a special dormitory, and some were paid for jobs that at most required minimal labor.

This public flaunting of higher learning's ideals infuriated many. "We go out after men for the sake of baseball and football, offering all sorts of inducements," said W.H. Andrews, the chancellor of Allegheny College not long after Penn State had beaten that Pennsylvania school's team 50–0 in 1904. "It isn't a thing unknown among us for a man to go from the football team of one college to the football team of another in midseason. Scholarships are offered to promising players. Professionalism is winked at."

By the early 1920s, it wasn't even being winked at. Penn State football, controlled by the alumni-dominated Athletic Advisory Committee, liberally handed out as many as 75 scholarships a year. Coach Hugo Bezdek was paid $14,500 in 1924, three times what the average faculty member earned and as much as PSU president Ralph Hetzel.

If you were an alumnus interested in victories, the system worked. Penn State football leaped into the national consciousness in 1923 when Bezdek's team earned an invitation to the Rose Bowl, where the Nittany Lions would fall to Southern Cal 14–3. From 1919–24, Bezdek's Penn State teams went 40–10, going undefeated two consecutive seasons (1920 and 1921).

But complaints that football needed to be restrained continued. Finally, in 1926, the Carnegie Foundation for the Advancement of Teaching commissioned Howard Savage, an educator who a year earlier had looked into athletics at British schools, to undertake a comprehensive study of American collegiate sports with football his primary focus.

At Penn State, an effort was made to move out in front of Savage's probe. Athletic Advisory Committee chairman Mike Sullivan suggested that by conducting its own investigation, Penn State could take early measures to correct some of the troubles Savage was sure to uncover.

School officials agreed and a special panel, the Beaver White Committee, was empowered. In March 1927, two years before Savage would issue his critical findings, the committee proposed four major changes to Penn State athletics.

First, the Athletic Advisory Committee should be disbanded and replaced by a board of athletic control that included more faculty, administration, and student members. Second, the new board should control all athletics. Third, the process of selecting alumni for the board should be revised. And fourth, all athletic scholarships should be phased out starting in the fall of 1928.

"[The] committee has become convinced that the present general system of athletic scholarships and financial help to athletes, in vogue in many collegiate institutions, is neither a credit to, nor in the best interests of, the institutions or good sportsmanship," the Beaver White report stated.

While many alumni were outraged, the reaction to the report on campus was surprisingly positive, especially among the group that might have been expected to oppose it most fervently—the students.

According to the terms of the Beaver White recommendations, the switch in control from the Advisory Committee to the Board of Athletic Control had to be approved by the students. The referendum, which essentially was a vote on all the proposed changes, passed overwhelmingly. By 1931, all the new measures were in place. There were no more scholarship athletes at Penn State.

Bezdek could read the tea leaves, so he stepped aside after the 1929 season. The man who replaced him was one of his assistants, a former Penn State All-American named Bob Higgins.

Born in Corning, New York, the brother of early birth-control advocate Margaret Sanger, Higgins struggled initially. His first team in 1930 went 3–4–2. A year later, the record was worse at 2–8 with Penn State failing to score a point in five of those losses. According to angry alumni, this was the inevitable result of no-scholarship football. "No boy wishes to become part of an institution which is the target of jokes and ridicule," wrote Charles Heppenstall, a 19th century Penn State player, in a 1931 letter to the *Alumni News*.

Soon agitated alumni began to circumvent the rules, supplying some financial aid on their own for football recruits. A 5–3 season in 1937 gave Higgins his first winning record. Though no one could have foreseen such good fortune then, the Nittany Lions' 3–4–1 record a year later would be their last losing season in 50 years. In the final decade of Higgins' tenure (1939–48), Penn State was a combined 62–16–7, with its 9–0–1 1947 team earning a spot in the Cotton Bowl.

With thousands more students—and in many cases their families—on campus, postwar attendance and interest increased for the football games at 14,000-seat Beaver Field. In 1946, Higgins' Nittany Lions attracted five-figure crowds to all their home games for the first time. And with victories over nationally recognized opponents like Navy, Pitt, and Washington State, demand stayed strong. In 1949, Penn State's trustees decided to more than double the size of the stadium, expanding its seating capacity to 30,000.

Ralph Hetzel had been Penn State's president in 1927 when athletic scholarships were banned. A vocal reformer, his presence squelched any decision about restoring them. It wasn't until his death in 1947 that a serious push was made to restore financial aid to athletes. Opponents argued that without scholarships the Nittany Lions had reached the 1947 Cotton Bowl and had been ranked No. 4 in the nation. But as scholarship supporters pointed out, that team was filled with returning war veterans, experienced and seasoned players in their mid-twenties, a quirk not likely to repeat itself.

When Higgins departed for health reasons at the end of the 1948 season, the pro-scholarship forces sensed an opening. In May 1949, two months after it authorized the Beaver Field improvements, the Athletic Advisory Board approved the introduction of 100 athletic scholarships, with 50 earmarked for football.

Higgins' exit also prompted a power struggle on a coaching staff already roiled by reports that the more recently hired assistants were being paid more than staff veterans. Two of

Higgins' ex-aides, Joe Bedenk and Earl Edwards, were the leading candidates to replace him. Each had his proponents, furthering the schism.

Edwards, the more popular among the assistants, lost out and left for Michigan State. Bedenk was hired but never won the loyalty of the Edwards backers, and despite a 5–4 record in 1949, Bedenk stepped down after that season, agreeing to remain as an assistant for his successor but concentrating on his role as head baseball coach.

Fearful that a perception of instability—three head coaches in three years—might impede the program's growth, Penn State administrators determined to require the new head man to maintain the existing staff.

Engle, as was his nature, was worried about those new aides, several of whom were still unhappy and none of whom had any experience with the Wing-T. Just days after he took the job, his old mentor, Harlow, was writing with advice as he would do for the next decade. "You will have a chance to adjust your coaches after you see them," the older man wrote. "Above all keep the confirmed Single-Wingers away from the varsity."

The shift in offensive formations was a godsend for Paterno, who despite his lack of coaching experience immediately became Engle's primary assistant and sounding board. "He was Rip's boy," said team trainer Ed Sulkowski.

Paterno had the advantage of knowing the system and the head coach. While the other assistants understandably were reluctant to challenge a recently hired superior, Paterno knew when he could push or question Engle. "They felt insecure, or at least watchful, until they got a handle on how to work with their new boss," Paterno said. His personal connection to Engle and his aggressive demeanor didn't immediately endear the young man to his colleagues.

Hiring a wet-behind-the-ears Brown graduate as one of just a handful of assistants was not as far-fetched as it might have appeared to them at first. Like the bulk of college football teams in that era, Penn State had used the Single Wing for decades. It was a run-heavy formation in which the ball was snapped to a tailback or fullback. The Wing-T Engle preferred was a variant of the increasingly popular T formation.

It differed from the standard T—the quarterback took the snap from center, with the halfbacks and fullback aligned behind him—in that one of the halfbacks would station himself on a flank. That variation not only opened up the field but allowed for more creativity, an aspect that appealed to both Engle and Paterno.

For all his brashness, Paterno exhibited some anxiety during his early days as a coach at State College. He had asked Engle for some specifics about how to learn on the job.

"I said to Rip, 'How do I coach? What's it take? Is there a course or something like that?' Rip handed me film," Paterno recalled. "He said, 'I'm going to give you three reels of film every day'—in those days we had 16-millimeter film—'and I want you to chart every single play on both sides of the football.' When I was done, he'd give me three more reels. I did that all summer. I finally started to realize what the game is all about. And I came back, and he said, 'What do you think? Are you going to be all right?' And I said, 'You know, I may be the best coach ever.'"

Engle also schooled his impatient protégé on how best to relate to players. He advised treating each one as an individual, since not all players were capable of the same responses or physical achievements; he should be willing to give them second chances; he should be prepared to answer any and all of their questions, and he always should remember that even though he was close to their age, he was their boss.

• • •

In the month between his hiring and his late-May arrival, Engle had purchased a home on Woodland Road in College Heights, a leafy tract of 300-plus Tudors, bungalows, and ranch houses adjacent to the northern edge of the campus. Since Engle's wife and son had not yet arrived, Paterno, who would one day buy a home in the neighborhood and raise his family there, slept in a bunk bed while Engle awaited his family and the rest of the furniture

Eventually, Paterno moved in with Steve and Ginger Suhey, a young married couple who lived in a two-bedroom apartment. The three became genuine friends, and the relationship didn't do any harm to Paterno's ambitions. The Suheys were well-connected. Steve had been an All-American for Higgins, who happened to be Ginger's father. The couple would have three sons—Larry, Matt, and Paul—and a grandson who played football for Penn State. "Through them," Paterno said of Steve and Ginger Suhey, "I was able to meet some younger people."

For Paterno, the transition from big city to small town was neither easy nor natural. He failed to sense the charms Engle had noted. His dismay was so profound that at one point during that initial season, Paterno told the coach to start looking for a replacement. "I'll go nuts in this hick town," he said.

He was, however, too antsy and inquisitive to sit through his suffering. The inherently social bachelor soon began to carve out a life away from football. He discovered that living so close to a large college campus had its benefits. He attended lectures and concerts, took classes in such subjects as the Australian novel and

Walt Whitman, and befriended graduate students and professors, particularly those who taught or were interested in literature.

Not surprisingly given his experiences at Brown, he found Penn State's teachers and students to be more approachable and more down to earth. He had dinner once a week with the other coaches. The rest of the time, if he weren't eating with the Suheys or in his room, Paterno opted for the local American Legion Hall, which had acceptable meals and one of the first TV sets in town.

In addition to the Suheys and his later landlords, fellow assistant Jim O'Hora and wife Bets, Paterno developed a small circle of friends. One, political science instructor Paul Litwak, provided the kind of lively intellectual conversation Paterno used to get at his family's dinner table. Most nights, though, Paterno was either watching game film, obsessing over the playbook, or reading. The days were long, but the work was fulfilling and he was beginning to enjoy himself.

The young coach's passion for football only intensified. Paterno didn't wear his trademark glasses when he got to State College, but he studied grainy film so long and so intently that his eyesight soon worsened. There were times when Paterno was such a football wonk that other coaches and players tried to avoid him, knowing that no matter the setting, the subject would soon turn to Xs and Os.

Quarterback Bob Scrabis recalled that Paterno often would attend PSU basketball games in Rec Hall, where several football players worked as ushers. At first, the young men would greet the assistant coach. But soon they learned not to, knowing Paterno quickly would direct the conversation toward football and ignore the event at hand. Scrabis said that during one of these off-the-field encounters, Paterno even suggested that when players ate dinner, they should shape their mashed potatoes into the form of a football to keep their minds on the game.

Paterno expected everyone else to share his devotion. Quarterback Milt Plum remembered walking across campus on the night before a game and encountering Paterno, who was a big believer in Friday night rest. "Get off your feet!" he yelled at the dumbstruck Plum. "Get off your feet!"

Paterno was ill-equipped to be a follower. Full of opinions and suggestions, he was not shy about expressing them, no matter the violations of pecking order or tact. "I was really a pain in the neck," he said. "I thought I was smarter than everybody else, and I had no patience for anyone who disagreed with me. I thought I had all the answers."

He once told Engle's popular wife, Sunny, to "shut up." On another occasion he got into athletic director McCoy's face, informing him, "We're going to win in spite of you." Dan Radakovich, a Penn State player who joined Engle's staff immediately after graduating in 1957, said the disagreements among Engle's aides sometimes got intense, but all parties gradually learned to leave their differences in the coaches' room. "They never carried over," Radakovich would say. "And nothing we discussed ever leaked out."

Assigned to work with backfield coach Frank Patrick in teaching the new system to the quarterbacks, Paterno didn't feel the need to take a back seat. "Joe never hesitated to speak his mind," O'Hora said. Patrick took it in stride, but others, particularly Bedenk, did not. The older coach called Paterno a "young whippersnapper."

But Engle knew how to handle his headstrong apprentice. "Even to Rip I was argumentative, cocky, frustrated," Paterno said. "I wanted him to get rid of people, make new things happen faster. While I moaned and complained, Rip held to his own way, which, in the long haul, proved to be the right way. I got away with being the whippersnapper I was because Rip always knew my goal was the good of the organization."

Obviously, since he would spend 16 years as Engle's assistant on a virtually unchanging staff, Paterno learned how to adapt, how to soften his grating nature, how to hold his tongue, and how to accept a point of view other than his own.

Penn State football historian Lou Prato contended Paterno survived his "brusque, headstrong, and combative nature... [through] a willingness to step back and analyze himself on a regular basis, especially when his decisions and motivations are criticized, and then to admit his own mistakes and short- comings, frequently using his instinctive, quick-witted sense of humor."

What also helped was his friendship with O'Hora, who became his landlord after the Suheys outgrew their apartment and moved. The easygoing son of Irish immigrants, O'Hora would become Paterno's buffer, mediating disputes between the youngest assistant and his older colleagues. "Without Jim O'Hora," Paterno said, "I never would have survived at Penn State.... He fought battles for me." And O'Hora paid a price. Initially after Paterno moved in with the older coach and his wife, the social life of the O'Horas slowed. Fearful that they might bring along their brash young tenant, some friends even stopped inviting the couple to join them for dinner or a movie.

Still, O'Hora stuck by Paterno and was the young man's landlord and mentor for nine years. O'Hora not only remained a close friend but served alongside or under Paterno for the next 26 years. "Of all the fine people Joe was fortunate to meet," George

Paterno said. "I think Jim O'Hora had the most dramatic and positive influence on him."

Joe Paterno could be sharp and demanding with those he coached, snapping and barking orders at them as if he were a 25-year veteran instead of a rookie assistant not much older than them. Perhaps because he was virtually a contemporary, some players resented Paterno's style, which was much more verbal and direct than they were used to. Some, however, saw past it, realizing there was a method to his madness. "He was an Ivy League-educated hustler," Charlie Pittman said.

Gradually, more and more players came around to Paterno's way. They didn't like it any better, but they saw its intent. "He could get on you pretty good, and a lot of guys weren't sure how to handle that," said Bob Mitinger, a Penn State star in the late 1950s. "But before too long guys started to understand that underneath it all he had our best interests at heart."

For all his annoying qualities, Paterno, as the Nittany Lions would learn, was sincere. He genuinely cared about them as players, students, and people. Without that ameliorating trait, it's doubtful he ever could have succeeded. "Players who play for him," one noted, "understand that he is an acquired taste."

Along with his football duties, Paterno had several off-the-field responsibilities. Knowing the kind of dogged student he had been, Engle asked Paterno to be the team's academic monitor. The young coach ran the study sessions, and he didn't just sit at a desk. He asked players constantly about their grades, their professors, the books they were reading. If he sensed a potential problem, he increased his vigilance. He wouldn't permit them to take "basket-weaving" courses or academic shortcuts. "We all learned pretty quickly that being a football player wasn't going to help us any in class," Mitinger said. "Rip and Joe made it clear that we were students first."

Then in 1951, Paterno would be assigned to the worst job of his long Penn State tenure. Engle made him the resident counselor for the football players, who were housed on the top two floors of McKee Hall.

If Paterno didn't oppose the concept of a players-only dorm from the start, he soon learned to, believing the social segregation made the youngsters feel "super special" instead of part of the university. He nagged Engle about it ceaselessly. In this case he got his way, and by 1952 the athletes were again living with the rest of the student population.

Paterno's quarterback tutoring would be essential in remaking Penn State's offense. Single-wing quarterbacks called the plays but did as much or more blocking as running and throwing. In the Wing-T, the quarterback would have to do all those things and more—because of the era's substitution rules, the quarterback would also have to play defense, so his mental acuity had to be nearly as sharp as his physical skills. Engle was convinced it would take a year to develop such a player. Paterno couldn't—and wouldn't—wait that long.

The quarterback Paterno focused on that first season was one of the ten returning non-scholarship players from 1949, Vince O'Bara. O'Bara had been a tailback in the Single Wing, but Engle saw in him some of the leadership and physical qualities he sought. Paterno took more convincing. "At first, I told Rip I didn't think O'Bara could be our quarterback," he said. That feeling was reinforced when O'Bara's first pass, in a Beaver Field win over Georgetown, was intercepted.

The Nittany Lions followed a season-opening victory with three straight losses—Army, Syracuse, and Nebraska. But both

O'Bara and the team improved quickly. Penn State won its final four games, including a 21–20 upset of Pitt at snowy Forbes Field, to finish 5–3–1. In his postseason assessments, Engle mentioned his young assistant's contributions, and for the first time Paterno the coach began to get some big-city newspaper attention.

• • •

As rapidly as he grasped Engle's offense, Paterno also took easily to recruiting. He could be charming and witty and had an easy way around people, especially with the parents of potential recruits. "He had the wonderful gift of making you feel at ease immediately," Bets O'Hora said.

But he could be as cunning and competitive as he was charming. For example, Paterno learned that if recruiters from other schools were in town, it was a good idea to keep the targeted athlete out of their range by taking him for a long ride or to dinner. He would hide players in hotel rooms. And he could close on a prospect like no one else. "He has been at it so long now that not many people remember what a tremendous recruiter he was," Conlin said. "If he went into a kid's house, it was pretty much game, set, and match."

There also are numerous stories of Paterno engaging in shouting or pushing matches with other coaches that he felt were venturing into his territory.

Beano Cook, the longtime ESPN analyst who was the sports information director for rival Pitt in the 1950s, remembered one such incident with Paterno at a Pittsburgh bar called Frankie Gustine's. "We got into an argument about a recruit that both schools wanted," Cook told the authors of the 2010 book, *They Know Joe*. "He made some derogatory comments about Pitt, and I gave it right back about Penn State. I'm lucky [PSU assistant

Sev] Toretti stepped in because the over/under on me with Paterno would have been 30 seconds."

The young assistant approached recruiting as thoroughly and as seriously as he did any other duty. Mitinger recalled how on a visit to Penn State he met with Paterno, who unbeknownst to the player had scouted one of his games. When Mitinger introduced himself, the coach said this formality wasn't necessary. "I know you," Paterno said. "You're No. 59 from Gaithersburg."

Those qualities plus Engle's fatherly presence and the avuncular nature of the rest of the staff helped Penn State fill its roster with new scholarship players. That first recruiting class would include such future stars as Rosey Grier, Jesse Arnelle, and Joe Yukica.

In the meantime, his colleagues were learning, slowly—and painfully in most instances—that while Paterno might have been noisy at meetings, he was always well-informed. It was clear to them that he knew football and equally clear that he knew what Engle wanted. "He was probably the best-prepared among the assistant coaches," O'Hora said. "He did his homework well."

O'Bara would be gone in Paterno's second season, so the young coach worked hard to familiarize Tony Rados, a Notre Dame transfer, with the quarterback position. Rados backed up Bob Szajna in 1951, and the Lions had another so-so 5–4 season. But as Rados learned the system and players like Arnelle, Grier, and Jim Garrity, the father of future Penn State star Gregg Garrity, matured, better times loomed.

Rados took over in 1952, and Penn State went 7–2–1, with losses to only Michigan State and Syracuse. Penn State shut out nationally ranked Pitt 17–0 and managed a 20–20 tie with a very good Purdue team. By then the schedule was beginning to include teams from beyond the East, typically at least one Big

Ten opponent a season. And players like Grier, who was from Georgia, reflected a more national scope in Penn State recruiting.

That same year Engle landed his first real superstar, convincing Reading (Pennsylvania) High running back Lenny Moore to come to Penn State. In doing so, Engle was following the advice of Harlow, who had advised him to "get a great running back." Paterno recalled, "[Harlow] said a great running back is somebody [who] when you put him in the secondary three times, you get two touchdowns."

That lesson was not lost on Paterno, who as a head coach would himself land a succession of great backs, including Curt Warner, D.J. Dozier, Lydell Mitchell, Franco Harris, John Cappelletti, Charlie Pittman, Curtis Enis, and Blair Thomas. Paterno could develop excellent quarterbacks, but he could recruit great runners.

Moore, the future NFL Hall of Famer whom Paterno would call "the best player I've ever coached, all-around," possessed the kind of breakaway ability the Lions offense had lacked. As he would prove with the NFL's Baltimore Colts, Moore could do anything. But at Penn State, he was slow coming out of the backfield on pass plays and the quarterbacks learned to look elsewhere. Moore had no such reluctance running the ball. "He could change direction in midair," Engle said. "No one could get a clean shot at him."

Moore played a pivotal role in one of the early signature victories of the Engle-Paterno era. It came against Syracuse on November 5, 1955. Syracuse was led by superstar running back Jim Brown. (Paterno likes to note that he once predicted that Brown, who would become perhaps the greatest professional runner ever, would never make it big in the NFL.) Brown's matchup with Moore created great anticipation, and Beaver Field was packed.

Moore ran for 146 yards and a touchdown on 22 carries. Brown, meanwhile, gained 159 yards on 20 carries, scored three touchdowns, caught two passes, kicked two extra points, ran back three kickoffs for 95 yards, and intercepted a pass. Still, Penn State won 21–20 in part because of the play of Plum, a strong-armed quarterback from southern New Jersey who had been nurtured carefully by Paterno.

The 1955 Nittany Lions finished with a 5–4 mark, but their record improved to 6–2–1 a year later with the losses coming to Army and Syracuse. The week of that Army game, Paterno's father died suddenly of a heart attack at 58. Paterno, who would miss the game, was stunned by the news. "Dad was a warm, wonderful human being who always saw only the best in people," he said. "He was always himself. Everyone who ever met him liked him."

It was not the only bolt from the blue—that year. As he shaved in the O'Horas' bathroom one morning, a bolt of lightning hit his bedroom. The house was damaged but spared, and Paterno always said it was fortunate he wasn't in bed at the time.

The two sobering events appeared to drive Paterno even harder to excel as if only by doing his best was he going to fulfill his father's faith in him and his own destiny.

Prato would say there was no more consequential game in the evolution of Penn State into one of the elite teams in college football than the 1956 road victory at Ohio State. Before a hostile crowd of 82,584 at Ohio Stadium, the Nittany Lions' 7–6 win earned them national headlines.

Woody Hayes' Buckeyes were 3–0, averaging 31 points and 333 yards of offense a game. Penn State, 2–1 with a loss to Army, was a three-touchdown underdog. The game was scoreless until a 72-yard punt by Plum set them up in Ohio State territory. Running back Bruce Gilmore scored from 1 yard out with 3:35 left in the fourth quarter. Ohio State drove down the field on a pair of long passes and scored its own touchdown. But on a successful PAT try, the Buckeyes were penalized for having too many men on the field. The post-penalty kick missed, and Penn State escaped with a narrow ego-boosting victory.

"Winning that game helped change the perception of Penn State in the eyes of the rest of the country," Radakovich said, "and especially the high school coaches. [Afterward] when our coaches went to see a player, instead of getting their second-best player, the high school coaches would show them their best player. In previous years, we'd say, 'Well, how about this kid?' And they'd say, 'Oh no, he's going to Michigan State,' or, 'He's going to Ohio State,' or, 'He's going to Purdue,' or something. So the Ohio State game was the turning point."

As Plum developed into a star, Paterno's influence in the coaches' room and his reputation beyond it continued to grow. He became more confident in his football knowledge, more willing to impart tips and strategy. He taught Plum a lesson that would become one of his own coaching cornerstones when he succeeded Engle, much to the annoyance of those critics who complained his offenses lacked imagination. If a play is working, Paterno told Plum, stick with it. If an off-tackle thrust gains 11 yards, run it again and again until the defense proves it can stop it.

Though Paterno was still not yet 30, when it came to the Lions' offense, his voice was loudest. As time went on, even Engle began to yield to his vision. "I'm not saying they argued," Plum said, "but it just ended up the way Joe wanted to do it. He sure as heck wasn't wishy-washy. It was, 'Here's the way we're going to do it. Let's go.'"

Al Jacks, a 1956–58 quarterback, said the offensive players had no doubt about who was in charge on their side of the ball. "It didn't take long for all of us to realize that [Joe] was running the whole offensive show," Jacks said.

While Plum was one of several good college quarterbacks Paterno helped train as an assistant, he was one of the few who also starred in the pros. Richie Lucas was a Heisman runner-up but enjoyed only an average career with the Buffalo Bills. Tony Rados, Pete Liske, Galen Hall, and many Nittany Lions quarterbacks after them were not even that successful. Was Paterno's tutelage the reason for their collegiate success? "We'll never know," Mitinger said, "but Joe was a very good teacher in one-on-one situations. I guarantee you that when some of those guys got to the pros, most of the coaches there didn't have the same kind of time—and maybe not the same kind of passion—to devote to them that Joe did."

The Nittany Lions went 6–3 in 1953 and kicked off a 7–2–1 season in 1955 with a victory over highly regarded and 17-point-favorite Illinois, which had future pros J.C. Caroline and Abe Woodson. Moore ran for 137 yards and intercepted a fourth-quarter pass as Penn State triumphed 14–12. Moore finished that season with a record 1,082 yards rushing—nearly double the previous mark—and Grier was one of the nation's best linemen on both sides of the ball.

Penn State got its first bowl bid in 12 years in 1959 after All-American quarterback Richie Lucas led them to an 8–2 regular season. In Philadelphia, a promoter named Bud Dudley devised a Liberty Bowl and got a television deal and a 100,000-

seat stadium to ensure its success. He couldn't do anything about the weather, though. On a cold and windy afternoon in Pennsylvania's largest city, only 36,211 fans turned out at Municipal Stadium to see Penn State defeat Bear Bryant's Alabama 7–0.

Engle loved trick plays. And on the final play of the first half, with Lucas injured and sidelined, Galen Hall took the snap on a field-goal try. It was a fake. Hall rolled out and hit Roger Kochman, who barely got into the end zone for the game's only score.

That Alabama win was nationally televised. As far back as 1949, Penn State football had appeared on television. Its October 1 game at Army that year was broadcast in New York City, though only a tiny percentage of the city's residents owned TV sets. A 1954 matchup with Penn at Franklin Field was broadcast. And in 1958, the Nittany Lions were again featured on a Saturday afternoon national telecast.

Penn State soon worked its way into the annual network rotation. In addition to the program Engle and Paterno were constructing, Mount Nittany and the area's colorful hills in autumn appealed to the broadcasters—even if most viewers were watching on black-and-white TVs. They seemed captivated by the place, helping to popularize Happy Valley as an apt synonym for State College and its environs.

Those same cameras also were developing a taste for the bespectacled Nittany Lions assistant who was so animated on the sideline and who chattered constantly alongside the more reserved Engle. Joe Paterno was good television, and from what the broadcasters had learned and repeated frequently to their millions of viewers, he was a pretty good coach, too.

6

LIKE SO MUCH OF AMERICA as the 1960s dawned, 33-year-old Joe Paterno was restless and full of questions. Before that tumultuous decade of riots, revolts, and raised consciousness concluded, the nation and the coach would undergo a painful and prolonged period of self-examination.

In 1960, after 10 years as Engle's assistant, Paterno remained uncertain about his future. While he felt sure he wanted to be a college head coach, he couldn't yet see where and when that might happen. As a result, the possibility of emulating his father and attending law school as a middle-aged man remained a comfortable, if increasingly unlikely, option.

Should he stay at Penn State with Engle? Would he be Engle's successor? If so, when? And if he did get a head job there or elsewhere, would he be able to manage a staff? Could he delegate authority? Change his mind? Keep quiet? If he failed, what then? It would be several more years before the answers began to appear.

By the time the 1960s ended in Woodstock's moonbeams and Apollo's moon landings, Paterno would have risen from near-obscurity to become a respected national figure, a married father of four who had proven he could assemble and guide an undefeated team, a man who publicly could challenge a U.S. president, and a coach who would be seen as the leading advocate for a set of college-football ideals that may never have existed.

The 1960s arrived with a yawn in State College. That the decade's excesses would come belatedly to State College wasn't surprising. Change proceeded slowly there. It was if Mount Nittany, which had served as a buffer against so much unpleasant weather over the centuries, protected the area from other torments, as well. A *Sports Illustrated* writer once described Happy Valley as "a time-warped Shangri-La of rocky meadows and russet leaves that moves along out of step with the rest of the world."

Penn State's middle-of-nowhere campus, with its Friday night bonfires, beanie-wearing freshmen, panty raids on McAllister Hall, fraternity housemothers, dress codes, and strict rules of behavior for dinner ("Don't play with the silver.") still resembled some Hollywood producer's outdated vision of college life.

Its students, the overwhelming majority white and middle-class, tended to be from small towns and were conservative in dress and outlook. Movie theaters and bars were closed on Sundays. There wasn't even a place to buy liquor in State College; thirsty students had to flee the dry town for "milk runs" to the closest state store in nearby Bellefonte. While the dismantling of collegiate institutions would become a hallmark of the 1960s, however, Penn State actually was ahead of the curve, even if the campus landmark it deconstructed was a football stadium.

Since 1909, Penn State's football home had been Beaver Field, a practical and unspectacular facility located near the heart of the sprawling campus and not far from Recreation Hall and the Nittany Lion Inn. Named for James Beaver, a Civil War hero from Centre County who went on to become Pennsylvania's 20th governor and the university's president, the stadium would be home to Engle's teams throughout the 1950s.

Its original wooden grandstands had been replaced by steel, and in 1949 its capacity had been expanded to more than 30,000. It was surrounded by a few brick ticket booths, and players changed in an adjacent water tower.

"It was a very close setting—almost like people were on top on you," said Galen Hall, a quarterback then and now a longtime Paterno assistant. "It was great. Everything was closed in at the old place, with all the trees and the water towers and the surroundings."

While it may have been intimate and charming, Beaver Field rarely was filled to capacity during the 1950s. But there were occasional hints of the popularity boom that was to come. For a November 7, 1959, game with rival Syracuse, for example, 34,000 fans—4,000 more than it could hold—filled the place.

As early as 1955, sensing the growing importance of athletics and recognizing the demographic surge the Baby Boom would soon create for colleges, athletic director McCoy had talked about a stadium upgrade. A native Pennsylvanian, McCoy had a radical suggestion. Instead of spending millions to replace or expand the existing structure, which was increasingly cramped by the growing west campus, why not dismantle it and move it east to an isolated spot near the agricultural fields?

There, he said, the facility could grow as needed, and modern amenities like parking lots could be more easily accommodated. McCoy even foresaw the tailgating that soon became a hallmark of game days there and elsewhere. "Eating out of the back of the car," he wrote in detailing his plans for administrators, "is ideally suited to parties coming to the campus from towns and cities within a 100-mile radius."

Eventually, the board of trustees agreed and the move was scheduled to occur after the 1959 season. Paterno, a traditionalist, seemed to be one of the plan's few critics, predicting to Engle that the shift to the remote locale would spell doom. "I said, 'You can't let them do that, Rip. It will ruin Penn State football,'" Paterno would recall. "We were close to the Nittany Lion Inn, and people were used to coming up there. We had a nice parking area across the street, where the golf course was, and the whole bit."

Though it had yet to prove its fan base could consistently fill a new and larger facility, Penn State, by most objective standards, was outgrowing its stadium. The postwar undergraduate population had exploded to more than 15,000. Those students, plus the faculty and the residents of surrounding towns—far removed from the professional sports life of Philadelphia and Pittsburgh—were increasingly devoted to Nittany Lions football.

The $1.6 million tinker-toy relocation project began immediately after 1959's final home game, a 46–0 rout of Holy Cross on November 14. Beaver Stadium would be disassembled into 700 pieces, trucked to the site along Curtin Road, then put back together again. When that was done, 16,000 seats were added, increasing its capacity to 46,284.

On September 17, 1960, the Nittany Lions played their first game at the new site, a 20–17 victory over Boston University before a crowd of 23,000 that easily could have fit into the old place. In fact, it initially appeared McCoy's vision might have been too grand. It would be two more years before the new Beaver Stadium had its first sellout—a homecoming game with Syracuse on October 20, 1962.

The football stadium wasn't the only significant change confronting Paterno in the early part of that decade. In 1961, O'Hora politely asked the longtime bachelor to abandon the room he had rented from him for nearly 11 years. O'Hora's family was growing, and he needed the bedroom.

Paterno had stayed there so long because he was a social being, one ill-equipped for solitude. "He could not be without people," O'Hora said. He also stayed because he was so devoted to football that single-bedroom living quarters sufficed. Had O'Hora not asked him to leave, Paterno admits, "I'd still be single."

With his Brooklyn accent, Italian roots, Ivy League tastes, and edgy personality, Paterno must have resembled an alien being to many of the small-town Pennsylvania girls who then inhabited the campus. But even if he hadn't seemed so odd, Paterno had little time for dating during his hectic early years in State College. He hadn't done much in Brooklyn or Providence either, though as a teenager he once dated Joe Torre's older sister. Not long afterward, she entered the convent, a choice Paterno jokingly insists their date inspired.

But sometime during the 1959 season, he had embarked on what would be his first serious relationship with a young student from western Pennsylvania named Sue Pohland.

One of the assistant coach's off-the-field duties at that time was monitoring the players' study sessions. Before and after each, he would see Pohland, a freshman when they first met. She was dating one of his players. Because that player was both talented and academically challenged, Paterno eventually approached her and asked her to keep an eye on his progress in school.

An honors student in English literature, Pohland soon learned that Paterno shared her interest in good books. When the boyfriend/player transferred and she and Paterno encountered each other at a campus lecture by literary critic Leslie Fielder, the relationship blossomed.

"No [it wasn't love at first sight]," she said in 2009. "He was telling me to keep studying. I said, 'Fine.' It took awhile." Like his mother, Pohland learned how to tap into Paterno's ambitions, how to nudge him in any direction. And, like him, she was curious, intellectual, and not afraid to speak her mind, all traits that appealed to the coach. '[We] discovered we both enjoyed the competition of disagreement," he said. Their dating would only inflame his dreams.

They continued to see each other, though more regularly after football season, and in the summer of 1961 the two vacationed separately at the New Jersey shore. There they would meet on the beach and enjoy long discussions about their favorite authors and the books they were reading. Before they returned to State College, Paterno, 13 years Pohland's senior, asked her to marry him. And on May 12, 1962, they were wed in her hometown of Latrobe, Pennsylvania.

Marriage didn't alter Paterno's football focus. Their planned two-month European honeymoon kept getting downsized, first to a few weeks in Bermuda, then to two weeks in the Virgin Islands…10 days in Florida…a week in Georgia…and finally to five days in Virginia Beach. En route to Virginia, Paterno stopped to see a recruit in Somerset, Pennsylvania. "We lost him to Miami," Paterno recalled.

Now married and with his understanding of football and college life growing keener each season, Paterno's desire to become a head coach intensified. As much as he enjoyed and benefited from his long apprenticeship with Engle, he longed to lead, to fulfill his destiny. Most of the others on the staff seemed content, perhaps because they knew each other so well but more likely because as tenured faculty they had a degree of job security.

Football-wise for Penn State, the decade couldn't have begun more positively. Engle's staff had stayed virtually intact since his hiring. Only ex–head coach Bedenk had left, departing in 1960. He was replaced by J.T. White, a former Michigan player, and White almost immediately meshed with his colleagues. "[Engle's] biggest strength over time," Conlin said, "has been the ability to keep that staff pretty much intact over the years. When you are working in a basic five-year talent cycle, the ability to have that kind of continuity helps in all areas."

Elsewhere, the stadium had recently been expanded yet again; the roster was filled with talent like ends Dave Robinson and Bob Mitinger, running backs Roger Kochman and Dick Hoak, tackle Charlie Sieminski, and quarterbacks Galen Hall and Pete Liske. The team had won its first bowl appearance in more than a decade, the Liberty Bowl in Philadelphia, which was played on December 19, 1959.

Curiously, that meeting with Bryant's all-white Crimson Tide provided an interesting contrast for Penn State. Compared to the dismal records at most other colleges, Penn State athletics had a rather enlightened tradition of race relations, even if few urban blacks were drawn to its rural location.

Cam Posey, the son of a wealthy Pittsburgh businessman who would go on to own black baseball's Homestead Greys, played basketball there in 1909. Blacks had been on the football team since 1941 when brothers Dave and Harry Alston made the freshman squad. Wally Triplett became the first African-American to start for the Nittany Lions in 1945. A year later, when reports surfaced suggesting the team's two blacks, Triplett and Dennie Hoggard, would not be permitted to perform there, the players voted to cancel a game in Miami.

In January 1948, Triplett became the first black athlete to play in the Cotton Bowl. And Penn State's blacks were, in that 1959 Liberty Bowl, the first Alabama would face. In a 1954 game against TCU in Forth Worth, Grier, Arnelle, and Moore became the first blacks to play there, although the team was forced to stay at a ranch 15 miles outside the segregated city.

Engle had coached African-Americans as far back as Waynesboro High. The star of his 1939 team there was James "Footsie" Brightful. But Waynesboro was near the Mason-Dixon Line, and Engle's team played two schools below it—Martinsburg (West Virginia) High and Hagerstown (Maryland) High. Those schools refused to play if Brightful did, and Engle acceded to their wishes.

Engle's views on race can't be discerned in retrospect, but it's hardly a stretch to suggest that Paterno, a relative progressive on the subject and one of his top recruiters, prodded the older man toward an increased recruitment of minorities.

Paterno's reputation would suffer in black communities in the 1970s and 1980s. His stated reluctance to exploit them, his adherence to strict academic policies, and the school's locale meant Penn State generally had fewer African-Americans than most opponents. Still, in the turbulent 1960s, Paterno was well-cast as a racial crusader. Angelo Paterno, after all, had been a prominent figure in New York's Interfaith Movement and had preached racial and ethnic tolerance.

Robinson tells the story of how a restaurant in Jacksonville refused him service before a Gator Bowl. The entire team left in protest, and Engle told them to find somplace to eat. But Robinson, shaken by the experience, was wary of going anywhere else. Sensing that, Paterno told the player to come with him and the two got a meal in a hotel coffee shop. "I would rather not have gone through those experiences," Robinson said. "But I did, and Joe helped me."

During his early years in State College, the Nittany Lions would land such black standouts as Grier, Arnelle, Moore, Robinson, and Charlie Janerette. And for a time, Engle's Penn State teams fielded more blacks than its opponents. However, like virtually every other school in that era, they seemed to be operating with an unofficial quota. As was so often the case in those early days of integration, Penn State's blacks invariably were stars. There didn't seem to be any room for them on college benches.

If the football team was diverse for that era, the rest of campus was not. Throughout the 1950s and 1960s, only a small percentage of Penn State's enrollment was black. As late as 1969, when Paterno was the head coach and black students occupied President Walker's office to express their dissatisfaction, there were fewer than 300 black students and only five on the faculty.

In his autobiography, Moore said that while Pennsylvania had a history of relatively good race relations, State College lagged behind. "Like Sisyphus, pushing his rock uphill for eternity, the issue of race struggles against a slippery slope of Eurocentric ideologies in the Central Pennsylvania town," Moore said.

• • •

That 1959 bowl victory over Alabama's powerhouse program had another impact. In a very real sense, it fixed Penn State permanently on the national radar. Absent from the final polls since 1954, that 1959 team would wind up 10th in the coaches rankings and 12th in the Associated Press poll. The Nittany Lions would finish in the top 20 each of the next five seasons and get invited to three more bowls—winning the 1960 Liberty again and the 1961 Gator before losing in the Gator in 1962.

It hadn't been easy for Engle's teams to push into the Eastern spotlight, such as it was. Without a major conference like the Big Ten, Big Eight, or Pac-8, football in the East was seen as a notch below other regions. "Schools in the East didn't get much respect," said Pete Liske, a Lions quarterback. "In the 1960s we tried to stretch a little bit and get some recognition [by scheduling more nationally known opponents]."

The school's locale was a little too remote for most New York and national writers to visit regularly. Army and Navy still got the lion's share of newspaper and television attention in the East. And Syracuse, with its succession of great running backs, was a perennial force.

But Engle's success couldn't long be ignored. Following the Liberty Bowl victory, Penn State would go 37–15 between 1960–64, finishing each of those five seasons with a national ranking. The 1960 team thumped Oregon in the second Liberty Bowl. The following season, the 8–3 Nittany Lions defeated Bobby Dodd's Georgia Tech in the Gator Bowl. A 9–1 regular-season record in 1962 resulted in another Gator Bowl bid. Though this time Florida would beat the Nittany Lions 17–7, Penn State wound up ranked No. 9, its best national standing since 1947.

Now writers from *Sports Illustrated* and other national publications began to check in regularly on Happy Valley. In October 1962, after Penn State dismantled Navy 41–7, *Sports Illustrated*'s Walter Bingham profiled Engle, noting that the coach hadn't had a losing season yet and that this Penn State team might be "one of the best in the nation."

As always, it was Engle's hangdog demeanor that intrigued the writer. When Bingham mentioned that Penn State had a streak of three straight season-ending bowl victories, the coach went ashen. "Around Penn State, Engle's gloom is taken about as seriously as a course in home decoration," Bingham wrote. "Were he to be playing Vassar on Saturday, he would try to convince people that his second team is weak and that Vassar had some good halfbacks."

Whether he meant to or not, Paterno learned that lesson well. He would annoy many throughout his career by painting even the softest of opponents as potential world-beaters. "That [fill-in-the-blank] is a good football team," went Paterno's weekly mantra. "If we're not ready to play, we're gonna get licked." Several of the national stories on Penn State quoted the bespectacled assistant who positioned himself next to Engle during games. Paterno's stature was growing. "His reputation started out slowly," historian Lou Prato said, "but once things got going around here, it picked up steam."

The contentiousness that marked Paterno's early relationship with the rest of Engle's staff had mellowed by the 1960s and to a surprising extent, transformed. The group became remarkably close. In a tradition that would carry over well into Paterno's head-coaching career, the Penn State aides all got together every Thursday night for drinks and dinner.

"They'd have cocktail parties at one of the coaches' houses and then go to dinner at the Tavern," Prato said. "When Joe was a bachelor and it was his turn to host the cocktail party, he'd have it in his little bedroom at the O'Horas. They all became really close."

Paterno enjoyed the camaraderie. "Thursday nights we used to say, 'The hay's in the barn,' and we'd go out and relax. We worked hard but...we had fun," Paterno said. "You found out you didn't have to get a good plate of spaghetti. After a couple of beers, it all tastes the same. And I got to like the people. I liked coaching."

On occasions they'd go to a play or a concert. There's a photo of the group on a Thursday outing at the Allenberry Playhouse in nearby Boiling Springs. It's a snowy night, and all of the other coaches are lined up alongside their wives. Paterno, the only bachelor, without his trademark glasses and decked out in a stylish overcoat, stands smiling and unattached in their midst.

Though most of his assistants drank—Paterno was developing a fondness for Jack Daniels—the teetotaling Engle didn't preach to them and wasn't uncomfortable being around them when they did.

Plum remembered that when he visited Penn State as a high school senior, he spent the night in a fraternity house where some of the students were drinking and smoking. The quarterback, who did neither, asked Engle if he were going to have to do the same to fit in at Penn State. "That's a decision you're going to have to make," Engle told him. "I don't drink, but I have a lot of friends who do and I enjoy being with them."

• • •

While it's difficult to pinpoint the exact moment when interest in Penn State football turned toward mania, the late afternoon and night of November 7, 1964, is a pretty good place to start. With quarterback Liske gone, the Nittany Lions struggled, dropping four of five to start the season. But even with so-so talent at quarterback (Gary Wydman) and tailback (Tom Urbanik) and not much of a passing game (end Bill Huber led the team with 25 catches), Paterno finally found some spark in the offense.

"Joe called me up one night after the third loss," Wydman recalled, "and basically said very simply, 'I'm not going to give up on you unless you give up on yourself.' As I look back on it, it was probably an important aspect for me to know somebody had confidence in me."

After a homecoming loss to Syracuse, Penn State trounced West Virginia and beat Maryland 17–9 before traveling to Columbus for another matchup with No. 2 Ohio State. Woody Hayes' Buckeyes were 6–0 and had allowed just 39 points all season. Despite Penn State's mediocre record, the two recent victories had reignited the passions of its student body. Since the game was on national television, students in State College crowded around TV sets in dormitory basements, fraternity houses, and bars.

Paterno personally game-planned the offense. The Nittany Lions played what Engle would afterward term "a perfect game." Ohio State could do nothing on offense, posting minus-14 yards in the first half and just 63 for the entire game. The Buckeyes didn't cross the 50 until the final quarter. The Nittany Lions, by contrast, ran up 349 yards and scored in each quarter. Said a somewhat stunned Hayes afterward, "It was the worst trouncing we ever got around here." He was right. No Ohio State team had ever been beaten so thoroughly at home. Penn State would win its final five games by a margin of 135–24.

The game's lopsidedness ignited the television viewers in State College. When it ended, an estimated 5,000 flooded the campus. Some hoisted a Volkswagen Beetle onto the lawn of President Walker's residence, and others dove into a campus pond.

The enthusiasm didn't diminish much the following week. When Penn State beat Pitt 28–0 that Saturday, a record crowd of 50,144—nearly 4,000 beyond its capacity—watched in Beaver Stadium.

• • •

As Paterno became a more familiar face and name, he would have numerous opportunities to make a lateral move to other staffs, but he stayed put out of loyalty to Engle and the genuine affection that had developed for the school and its surroundings.

Paterno had a persistent feeling that one day he could bend Penn State's program to his coaching ideals, especially since those ideals seemed to mesh so neatly with the university's.

Despite his attachment to Penn State, he almost certainly would have left for the right destination, the right price, and the right situation. But something always kept him from going. He turned down chances to become an NFL assistant in Cleveland and in Baltimore where Engle's onetime Brown assistant, Weeb Ewbank, was now the Colts' head man. But in the late 1950s, Paterno had been disappointed when Engle rejected an offer from Southern California.

Paterno had wanted to go along to Los Angeles. When the head coach polled his eight assistants on how they felt about a possible move there, Paterno was the only one in favor of relocating. Not only was USC a more glamorous name in college sports, but a move to the West Coast would have allowed him to experience a new challenge, a new atmosphere. And from spotlit L.A., he knew, landing a head-coaching job would be a cinch. When Engle decided to stay put, White recalled, "Joe was furious."

The details leading to Engle's retirement and Paterno's ascension—the who, what, when, where, and why—have been obscured by the fog of time. Paterno alone survives among the key figures. As a result, a somewhat fuzzy picture remains of what would be the most significant decision in Penn State history.

A chronic worrier whose health suffered during each season, Engle had been thinking of walking away as early as 1962. "Once you reach 55, you have to work harder and harder to get the job done," Engle said later. Some close to the program also had noticed that as the 1960s wore on the coach's mind didn't seem as sharp as it once had been.

If Engle had been vascilating about exactly when to step aside, the 1965 season must have convinced him. Engle's Nittany Lions finished with a 5–5 mark, the poorest of his career there and the team's worst since 1938. Due to turn 60 the following March, Engle finally made the decision to leave sometime after the summer of 1965. "[He] was wearing out," said his son, Chip. By then, Paterno already had his foot well in the door.

Late in 1964, after Yale's coach John Pont left for Indiana, the Ivy League school offered Paterno the job. Yale had tried before in 1963. Then, Paterno had sought counsel from Engle who told his assistant Yale might be the perfect fit. Even if he didn't win there, Engle pointed out, the school's powerful alumni could make him a rich man.

Pont eventually got the job. "They told me they were going to give the job to Pont because it was late and he could bring his whole staff with him," Paterno said. But when Pont departed Yale in 1964 after just two seasons, Paterno was contacted again. He got the call at a banquet in Philadelphia. The long ride back to State College allowed him plenty of time for thought.

Once again, he was sorely tempted. The prospect of experiencing a more vibrant cultural and intellectual scene at the prestigious New Haven school appealed to him. And with running back Calvin Hill and quarterback Brian Dowling, Yale was experiencing renewed football glory, though it would be its last gasp.

Paterno by then understood the days were over when schools like Yale could contend for a national title. That was guaranteed by the Ivy League's creation in 1954 and when the eight private Northeastern schools voted to eliminate athletic scholarships.

Wearying of waiting after 15 seasons as an assistant and apparently unsure of Engle's intentions, Paterno wisely used this latest offer as a bargaining chip. When word of Yale's interest leaked to the press, Paterno was coy, saying he would have to discuss the matter with his wife and "some others." It had seemed clear to everyone for some time that Paterno was Engle's heir apparent. Still, he intended to find out for sure.

The coach would say later, and repeat over the years, that he first went to Engle and McCoy. While neither provided him with an ironclad guarantee, they assured him he was the front runner. To emphasize that fact, they gave him the title of associate head coach, which further distinguished him from the rest of Engle's staff.

George Paterno, whose otherwise entertaining book is riddled with factual errors, contended that McCoy's assurance to his brother was stronger than that. "Ernie...promised [Joe] that when Rip retired, if he was still Athletic Director, Joe would get the job. Joe grasped Ernie's strong hand and they shook on the agreement."

According to George Paterno, Joe still had doubts since ultimately the hiring of a head coach would have to be approved by the university's president and the trustees. George also wrote that since Joe Paterno was an Italian Catholic in a university culture dominated by German Protestants, their approval was far from a certainty.

Whether or not his ethnicity was a major concern, Paterno surely was wary. He had watched another Italian from Brooklyn, Vince Lombardi, get passed over for head-coaching jobs at Fordham, Minnesota, Wake Forest, and Virginia, even though Lombardi had amassed an impressive resume as an assistant at Army and with the New York Giants. When Paterno asked Lombardi why he thought he'd been snubbed, the older man told him there were two reasons. "I'm Catholic, and I'm Italian."

Paterno approached Walker with his concerns. According to the coach's autobiography, the president told Paterno, "If you're good enough, you'll get the job." Though that might sound like a less-than-ringing endorsement of an assistant who had proven himself capable over a decade and a half, Paterno apparently was appeased.

A half-century later, Engle's son, Chip, told a much different story to authors Neil Rudel and Cory Giger for their book, *They Know Joe*. According to Chip's version, Rip Engle went to McCoy for the AD's imprimatur on Paterno's new title as well as to get some formal guarantee that his longtime protégé would succeed him. When McCoy balked, Engle sought a meeting with Walker.

Walker, the younger Engle claimed, summoned the men to his office and asked the head coach if he thought Paterno was ready and capable. "My dad said, 'Yep. Definitely,'" Chip Engle recalled. "Eric Walker turned to Ernie and said, 'Take care of that, Ernie.' So Ernie was overruled.... My opinion on it—and it's strictly my opinion—is that Ernie McCoy was a control freak, and he didn't want anybody telling him what to do."

Though Paterno has always insisted administrators never promised him anything, it's difficult to imagine he would have stayed so long at Penn State, turning down Yale and several other appealing offers without some kind of formal acknowledgement that he would be Engle's successor.

In any event, the news that Paterno was staying and getting a loftier title validated what sportswriters, alumni, and fans already believed—that he would replace Engle, probably sooner rather than later. But power and succession are sensitive subjects, and just a few days before Engle's retirement was made public, he and Paterno reacted negatively to a story on the subject.

Lou Prato, now Penn State's football historian but then a freelance writer for *Pittsburgh Sports Weekly*, wrote in an issue dated February 21, 1965, but released the previous week that

Paterno had been holding the program's reins for some time. Because Penn State's 5–5 season gave some alumni pause about Paterno, the writer defended the younger coach.

His page six column was headlined "Raps Against Paterno Are Unjustified." "For years now," Prato wrote, "it has been universally accepted that Joe Paterno will be the head football coach at Penn State upon the retirement of Rip Engle. Penn State alumni in particular have heartily endorsed the idea. After all, they say, hasn't Paterno run the show for years? Recently though some folks have been having second thoughts about the wisdom of promoting Paterno."

The coaches saw the article and sometime during the week of February 13, when Prato and his wife were eating dinner at their Harrisburg home, Engle phoned. "I'd always had a good relationship with Rip," Prato recalled. "He wasn't angry as much as he was sorry about the whole story. He thought it made him look bad. It was like, 'How could you write this? It made me look bad.'" In an awkward position, Paterno apparently was upset for the same reason.

What likely annoyed them as much as the content was the article's timing. It appeared just days before news of Engle's departure would be made public, jeopardizing what the principals undoubtedly had hoped would be a tranquil transition.

A few days later, on the 11:00 PM newscast of Pittsburgh's KDKA-TV, Tom Bender, who also was the play-by-play man on Penn State football broadcasts, broke the story of Engle's departure, citing "a private source." At 12:30 PM the following day, Penn State confirmed the report but did not yet identify Engle's successor.

That night Engle was the guest speaker at a sports banquet at Meyersdale Area High School, not far from his boyhood home.

He acknowledged that he would be departing. "Sunny and I have been thinking about this for a long time," he said. Someone in the audience interrupted Engle to tell him he'd heard a report that said Paterno would be his replacement.

If that weren't the case already, it soon would be. That Friday, following Bender's scoop, McCoy summoned Paterno to his office. Paterno later wrote, "[McCoy] said, 'Do you want the job?' I said, 'Yeah.' He said, 'Okay.' We shook hands, and he said, 'You get $20,000 a year.'"

A press conference was scheduled for Saturday to introduce Penn State's 14th head football coach. The switch would become official with the coming of the next fiscal year on July 1, which would turn out to be the same day Paterno's third child, David, was born.

Except for the news that he would retain all of Engle's staff, the Paterno half of the story was so unsurprising that it created little buzz in State College or beyond. Longtime assistants often replaced retiring coaches. Left unsaid was the fact that they also often failed.

Paterno was 39, an advanced age for a first-time college head coach. Only one of the 10 men he would face in his inaugural season—Pitt's Dave Hart—had waited longer

"It will be an impossible task to replace Rip's inspiration and leadership," Paterno said at the news conference. "However, if hard work and dedication can succeed, then I'm certain our staff will develop good and exciting teams."

With 16 years of ideas to implement, he could hardly wait to get started. "I wasn't sure then how good a head coach I could be," he said. "But I was damn sure I'd find out pretty quick, not stagger around for four or five years. I'd made up my mind in a hurry about that."

7

As a fervent fan of Aeneas, the mythical creator of the Eternal City, Joe Paterno knew as well as anyone that Rome was not built in a day. Neither is a legend, at least not one that would prove as deep and enduring as Paterno. St. Joe, the dragon-slaying knight in blue-and-white armor, would not emerge fully formed for another decade and a half. And as with any popular legend, this one would require a moral core, heroic action, a compelling victory, and eager storytellers.

Its foundation had been established before the 1960s ended. Penn State's coach already was preaching his message of reform, jousting with the growing colossus of college sports. By then he had several dramatic and important victories on his resume, none more significant than winning the hearts and minds of sportswriters.

Sportswriters, as much as gifted recruits, were an immediate Paterno target when he took over in the winter of 1966. While Penn State had been featured frequently in *Sports Illustrated* by then and appeared often on national television, there was practically no sense, not even in its home state, that this was an elite national program, one that could turn an entire populace to mush on Saturdays like an Alabama or Texas. "When I went

95

there, Penn State did not have the reputation it has now," said Dennis Onkotz, one of Paterno's first All-Americans.

While local newspapers sent reporters and photographers to the Nittany Lions games, there was little day-to-day coverage and none of the constant, probing attention that soon would be a hallmark of sports journalism. The newspapers in Harrisburg and around the State College area, plus the student-run *Daily Collegian* and the wire services kept an eye on Penn State football, but not many other news organizations did. There wasn't yet much local television in Centre County. Games were broadcast, but the school's sports radio network was still in its infancy. And State College was too isolated to attract daily interest from other newspapers, even those in the state's largest cities.

Engle's media approach had been traditional. Those reporters who bothered to show up were welcome at practices. His office door was open, and he was accessible. Difficult as it may be to imagine now in this all-day news environment, Engle actually communicated with some journalists via mail, his secretary typing out his answers to their written queries. With no other example, Paterno began his tenure in much the same way.

"Practices were wide open," Prato recalled. "Joe was friendly to everybody. He was a nice guy to the young reporters. Of course, we were a different breed of cat. We weren't always looking for dirt."

But in the back of his mind, the coach intended to manage closely the release of information to shape his program to his outlook. Until he was in his seventies, Paterno genuinely enjoyed the company of writers. However, he gradually pulled back on their access. Practices would be closed. Little would be said about game plans or injuries. Assistants and players would, with few exceptions, be off-limits. He wasn't going to be antagonistic, but he alone would set the agenda. Before he could do that, though, he needed to cultivate relationships.

Along with Jim Tarman, the sports information director who would go on to become the university's athletic director and one of his closest friends, Paterno devised a clever and aggressive public-relations strategy.

Sportswriters, he knew, enjoyed free booze even more than free food. So Paterno and Tarman decided to pack a suitcase full of liquor and travel the state and, to a limited extent, the East, oiling the media wheels with alcohol. During that first off-season, they would visit Philadelphia, Pittsburgh, Allentown, Erie, Reading, and Scranton in Pennsylvania, as well as Baltimore, Trenton, and New York City. At each stop, they'd rent a hotel room and using whiskey, bourbon, and vodka as bait, they would invite the local writers to meet Penn State's new coach and hear his message.

"We went to the Warwick Hotel in Philadelphia, pulled up to the [front], and the valet comes and asks if we had any luggage," Paterno recalled of one such trip. "We said, 'Yeah, there's one in the back,' and it's this box packed with booze. He goes to pick it up and says, 'What do you have in here? Weights?' We had a lot of fun, and it gave us a chance to talk Penn State football, which we needed."

The cocktail excursions worked so well that Paterno, with a few tweaks, adapted them to his in-season routine. On game-week Fridays, after days of frenetic preparation, the coach liked to relax. He and Tarman invited those writers who journeyed to State College for off-the-record cocktail sessions, first at Tarman's house and later in Paterno's basement. For road games, the gab sessions would take place in Penn State's hotels.

The regular 10 to 12 attendees at what one would call "intimate affairs" were impressed by Paterno's ability to charm. Many of them shared his passion for books and ideas. "He felt qualified to talk on any subject that came up," Tarman said.

Fueled by the liquor, recalled Ralph Bernstein, the late head of the Associated Press sports bureau in Philadelphia, those subjects ranged "from politics to science to sports to sex." The drinking and the discussions could go on for hours—though the coach usually left at 10:00 PM to join his sequestered team.

The sportswriters were struck by how different Paterno was from their conventional image of a football coach. This was no growling Woody Hayes, no slick John Mackay, no lumbering Duffy Daugherty. This was something new and intriguing. They couldn't write enough about him.

The relationship proved symbiotic. While the writers were privy to Paterno's off-the-record thoughts and strategies, infusing their copy with a certain authority their editors loved, the coach was promoting his team and trumpeting his philosophy.

Frequently the conversation turned to abuses, real and perceived, in college football. In the 1960s alone, there had been a major point-fixing scandal in college basketball, a controversial investigative piece by the *Saturday Evening Post* about an alleged cheating incident that involved Alabama's Bryant and Georgia's Wally Butts, and numerous incidents about the ongoing subsidization—academic and financial—of athletes.

Using his own experiences at Brown as a model, Paterno spoke out loudly and often. Football players, he said, should be challenged in the classroom as well as on the field. These youngsters needed to be nurtured and molded, not coddled and exploited. This oft-stated vision, suffused with wit, passion, and quotations from Shakespeare and Homer, impacted his audience whether they be sportswriters, fans, or the parents of recruits.

Bill Conlin, a writer for the *Philadelphia Bulletin* and later that city's *Daily News*, was a regular attendee. He labeled Paterno's quest for harmony between athletics and academics the "Grand Experiment." An easy way to summarize the coach's reform philosophy, the name stuck.

"He resented the 'Cow College' label," Conlin said. "He wanted to recruit athletes who could win with their minds as well as their bodies, who would not only graduate but have fulfilling lives after football."

Paterno was an Italian from Brooklyn. As was the case when he was a young assistant, he needed no prodding to express an opinion. On July 28, 1966, nearly two months before he'd even coached his first game, he wrote a guest column for the *Centre Daily Times*. After decrying college sports' excesses, he lamented that "the power to determine goals and policies and to make decisions rests in the hands of alumni, booster clubs, friends of the 'establishment,' or perhaps business entrepreneurs." He made it clear—then and ever after—that Penn State did not operate that way. Many welcomed his criticism as courageous and necessary, while others, particularly some of his fellow coaches, found it brash and self-serving.

Whatever. Paterno had found his aria. And he would never stop singing.

• • •

The writers were drawn to the Grand Experiment side of Paterno's personality—the reasoned, rational, even charming nature that he inherited from his father. What wasn't always in plain sight to them or others outside the program was his mother's gift of combativeness. Despite the halo that adoring writers quickly and eagerly placed atop "St. Joe's" head, he'd gotten a healthy dose of that trait.

"I'm not the kind of guy who's going to be content winning five, six games a year," Paterno said. "I mean, I want to win them all. Winning isn't everything, but it's the most important thing. I think that's the attitude you have to bring to it."

Jim Tarman described in even starker terms how fiery his friend could be in his early head-coaching days. "He was terribly intense in his desire to win," Tarman said. "I think there was a time when he probably would have done almost anything to win."

That attitude, so contrary to his image, made his first season as head coach extremely difficult. Engle's final team had gone 5–5, and Paterno came to the job flush with ideas on how to improve on that. He had changes he wanted to implement, though they didn't include his staff, which had stayed intact through the years.

Their ranks grew by one in 1960 when Radakovich was hired to coach the linebackers. George Welsh arrived in 1963. When Sev Toretti left to assume the role of recruiting director for the burgeoning program, Joe McMullen replaced him. Finally, to fill his old assistant's role, Paterno chose Western Pennsylvania high school's coach Bob Phillips in 1966.

In charge now for the first time, Paterno's interplay with his aides and players changed. Though he'd been preparing for leadership his entire life, the transition after 16 years with Engle initially proved problematic. Sitting behind his new desk in Rec Hall, Paterno's certainties morphed into doubts, doubts led to questions, and the questions kept him up at night.

How much should he change Engle's successful system? How heavily should he rely on his assistants' counsel? When did he adopt their ideas? When did he overrule them? Should he be more authoritarian? More fraternal? A CEO? In that first season and beyond, Paterno struggled to find a comfortable leadership style. And still he watched more film, devised more plays, and practiced longer hours.

The angst exacerbated some of his more unpleasant traits, the same ones he'd displayed as Engle's young aide-de-camp. He could be arrogant, brash, and condescending, though few at the time recognized them as the ABCs of self-doubt. "When I got here," said Fran Ganter, who came to Penn State in 1967 to play for Paterno and would stay as an assistant until 2004, "Joe was a strictly a dictator."

Paterno would later call that 1966 season "the darkest" year of his life. Not one of the darkest—*the* darkest. That assessment is even more striking when you consider it was offered from the perspective of two-plus decades later when one would assume he had ample time to heal and forget.

It all began officially on September 17, 1966, when the Nittany Lions played their first game, against Saban's Maryland, in front of a Beaver Stadium crowd of 40,911. Engle had not left Paterno devoid of talent. Bob Campbell was a strong runner. Quarterback Jack White was returning. Ted Kwalick, who had played for Phillips at Montour High near Pittsburgh, would develop into Penn State's best tight end. And an otherwise thin defense was anchored by safety Tim Montgomery and linebacker Mike Reid, the soon-to-be tackle/concert pianist who would come to epitomize the best of his coach's Grand Experiment.

Reid was everywhere against Maryland, causing three safeties in a contest Penn State would win 15–7. It was a good start, but hardly one that satisfied the coach's perfectionist side. He had installed a new formation, the Power-I, and it looked disjointed.

He was embarrassed. And so, as it turned out, was Maryland's Saban, in his first and last opener with the Terrapins.

"I ran over to see Lou but couldn't find him so I went home dejected," Paterno said. "Later Lou called to apologize, saying we both coached so lousy he didn't have the heart to congratulate anyone."

More reasons for dejection would soon follow. A week later, the Lions traveled to No. 1–ranked Michigan State, which that season had one of the most talent-rich teams in college history.

In an era when several southern conferences were still segregated and northern schools proceeded with caution on integration, the Spartans were an anomaly. Most of MSU's stars were African-Americans—quarterback Jimmy Raye, running back Clint Jones, and wideout Gene Washington on offense, plus linebacker George Webster and mammoth lineman Bubba Smith on defense.

In its "Game of the Century" matchup with Notre Dame later that season, Michigan State would start 12 African-Americans, while the Irish started one. In terms of race and talent, Michigan State stood in sharp contrast to most of its opponents—including Penn State, which had only a handful of blacks on its roster and little chance in this matchup.

The Spartans ran away with a lopsided 42–8 triumph. Paterno had tried to use a pass-coverage scheme he'd installed late that week, and it looked it. Michigan State overran and outran the Nittany Lions, who appeared positively lead-footed in comparison. "We took a hell of a licking," Paterno said.

The lessons of that loss, however, were not wasted on the 39-year-old coach. In the future, any new wrinkles would be worked on early in the practice week. And the influx of blacks into college sports—a trend that would accelerate after Texas

Western's all-black starting five upset Adolph Rupp's all-white Kentucky in the NCAA basketball championship earlier that same year—caused Paterno to reevaluate further. In a sport historically built on power, he began to talk about the need for more speed on both sides of the ball.

A week later, at Army, the defense was slightly improved, but the Power-I was a no-show again. The Cadets' ugly 11–0 win sparked criticism during the game and later of the new coach and especially his offense.

"During that game when they got beat by Army," Prato said. "[AD] Ernie McCoy said very loud in the press box that if Joe didn't change the offense, 'We'll be looking for a new coach.' A couple of assistants heard that and went down and told Joe. Joe [who had clashed with McCoy before and would again] said he'd been planning to change it anyway but that he wasn't going to change it just because McCoy wanted it done."

Paterno made other changes, subbing Tom Sherman for quarterback Jack White, who had nearly been maimed by Smith in the Michigan State loss. Things got better momentarily with a 30–21 home win over Boston College. But the following week came a second blowout loss in a month—in this instance, a 49–11 thrashing at No. 4 UCLA. "We weren't going to win that game," Paterno said. "But we shouldn't have been beaten that badly. We couldn't do anything right."

The rout—coupled with a feeling that UCLA coach Tommy Prothro, whose team tried a late-game onside kick, had wanted to run up the score, and a suspicion that the Bruins were radioing signals to quarterback Gary Beban—had Paterno stewing on the long flight home.

The stresses wouldn't stop. No wonder Engle had developed stomach problems. Not only was McCoy on Paterno's back, but so were sportswriters. In addition, some of his players, pushed to their limits by an overeager new coach, were grumbling so loudly that he heard it.

Fans, their expectations inflated by the success of Engle's teams in the first half of the decade, were getting antsy, too. Paterno was getting hate mail, and cranks were telephoning his home since his number was in the phone book, as it still is today. He faced an avalanche of advice and criticism that initial season. Worse, he was trying to absorb it all.

When one alumnus, a physician from East Stroudsburg, Pennsylvania, wrote to tell him how disappointed he was in the football at his alma mater, Paterno testily responded: "If you have any suggestions, bring the people down and I'll be glad to talk to them." That prompted the now-agitated grad to write a nasty reply. Finally, in yet another letter, Paterno urged him to relax. "If I can't do the job here, I'll be the first one to know it." It was the intemperate reaction of an insecure coach, and Paterno knew it.

"I think I was frantic to cover a fear that after 16 years of working and waiting to be head coach, I wasn't going to be able to deliver, that I might not be as good as I wanted to think I was," Paterno said.

What might happen if things got worse? Would he be demoted? Fired? If so, would he ever get another chance as a head coach? Sure there was always law school, but he was 39 and even if he did go, how would he support his young family? (By the time the 1966 season started, he and Sue had three young children—Diana was born in 1963, Mary Katherine in 1965, and David the previous July.)

So he responded the only way he knew, by driving himself even harder. Penn State went back to a version of the Wing-T, and the offense gelled in two psyche-saving victories—38–6 at West Virginia and a 33–15 homecoming win over California.

Hard-fought but not unexpected losses to Syracuse and Georgia Tech followed. With a final-game win over Pitt, Paterno's first season concluded with the same so-so 5–5 record as Engle's last. It was a disappointing but evenly balanced mark upon which the still-uncertain coach's future teetered.

The summer would be hard and hot as Paterno examined everything about the foundering program. He was difficult to be around, snapping at people in the office and at home. A surer indication of his anxiety might have been the long silences. Normally loquacious, Paterno tended to go mute when his mind was deeply engaged. The more severe the problem he confronted, the more profound his silence. The former honor student retreated into a football cocoon, attacking his task determinedly and alone, desperately trying to raise a C-minus to an A.

The week-to-week grind of football left little time for anything but changing course. He joined the family for hastily consumed meals and then went back to work. He studied film endlessly in a makeshift upstairs office at the tiny home the Paternos had purchased in State College's Park Forest neighborhood. He drew up new plays, recruited, revised, re-worked, reconsidered.

"He didn't used to be able to handle losing," Sue Paterno said seven years later, by which time her husband rarely had to. "He'd shut the door and not come out. He was a real S.O.B.... After his first year as head coach in 1966, the team was 5–5 and he was despondent. He spent the whole summer planning a new defense. Oh, that was rough, keeping the kids out of his hair and all. He said that if he didn't have a winning season the second year, he would quit and go back to assistant coaching. He said it wasn't fair to the kids to be coached by a loser."

The summer of soul-searching would produce tangible results. Paterno realized he'd been too tough on his players. "I had become so demanding that everybody was unhappy," he said. His father had urged him to "have fun," and Engle had reminded him that, "This is their team, not ours," Paterno vowed to loosen up in 1967, to try to get to know players as people, and to learn what inspired and frightened them.

A dozen years earlier, Paterno recalled, Lombardi had told him much the same thing. Coaches who could draw up great plays on blackboards were a dime a dozen, the older man counseled Paterno over lunch. "The ones who win," Lombardi said, "get inside their players and motivate them."

He did that. Strategically, Paterno installed a new 4-4-3 defense, a revolutionary concept at the time and one the coach has always insisted took opponents four or five years to decipher. Great linebackers were essential to the scheme, whose demands for flexibility required them to be strong, swift, and smart. He began hunting for some, and he would find them.

• • •

The new Paterno didn't last long. The facade he'd constucted that summer began to evaporate when the 1967 season started in Annapolis, Maryland, on September 23. Penn State suffered a disheartening 23–22 loss to Navy that day. The Nittany Lions had grabbed a 22–17 edge late in the fourth quarter when Tom Sherman and Bob Campbell connected on a 20-yard scoring pass. But the Midshipmen came right back against the 4-4-3, driving 78 yards in the closing minutes. The winning touchdown pass was caught by Navy's Rob Taylor. It was Taylor's

10th reception of a game in which Penn State's bigger, more athletic defense would yield a disturbing 489 yards.

The defeat meant that Paterno—though it would be the last time in his long career—had a sub-.500 career coaching mark at 5–6. He was embarrassed and furious, calling the Navy loss "the shabbiest game I've ever been a part of." Once again his insecurities caused him to lash out unwisely, this time in the postgame locker room where he harangued his defenders for being too soft.

What really prompted the explosion, he later admitted, was a fear that his new defense, like his sagging career, might be a flop. Paterno was a longtime offensive coach, so the players on that side of the ball had found it easier to make the transition from Engle to Paterno. It was different on defense, however, where many of the returnees doubted that their new coach knew what he was talking about.

The silent Paterno resurfaced on the ride back to State College. In his traditional spot in the first bus' right front seat, the coach stared out the window for much of the 150-mile trip, pondering his schemes, his team, and his future. "I was having my doubts," he said. "We were terrible."

Maybe all his optimism had been misplaced. Perhaps Penn State would never be anything more than a good—and sometimes very good—Eastern team. Nothing so far suggested otherwise. In three games against recognized national powers—Michigan State, UCLA, and Georgia Tech—his Nittany Lions went 0–3 and were outscored 112–19.

Maybe he needed to expand his recruiting geographically and racially. Michigan State, with all its black talent, much of it from the Deep South, had looked like an NFL team compared to the Lions. If that was the solution, Paterno would have to figure out how to attract more blacks, many of whom had come from subpar schools and had personal problems in their pasts, while maintaining the standards he'd been promoting in his Grand Experiment.

Privately, Paterno thought Penn State could help by initiating a program to assist disadvantaged students in gaining admission. In his mind, such a plan wouldn't result in academically unqualified students on his team; it would instead help them qualify and meet his standards. Not yet powerful and persuasive enough to demand such a change, Paterno asked a friendly reporter to plant the idea in one of his columns. The sportswriter complied. By the early 1970s, there was a new Penn State president, John Oswald. When Oswald, a social liberal, led the University of Kentucky, he had urged Adolph Rupp to recruit black players for the basketball team. He liked the idea and began to take steps to implement it at Penn State.

By then, Paterno had made some headway in convincing top black athletes to come to Happy Valley. Charlie Pittman was a running back on the 1967 team, and Jim Kates was a linebacker. The next year Paterno would add Lydell Mitchell and Franco Harris, a pair of African-American runners from southern New Jersey who would help lead the Nittany Lions to new heights.

Meanwhile, on the trip back from Annapolis, some of the younger Nittany Lions in the back of the bus were as puzzled as their coach. These youngsters, who soon would be the core of Paterno's breakout teams, wondered why they weren't yet on the field. They could see in practices that they were better than several of the upper-classmen starters, and they couldn't understand how their coach could miss it.

"We had some really good young players," said Dennis Onkotz, a sophomore linebacker who was one of them. "We had some sophomores—in those days freshman were not eligible—that were good players. And I said to myself, 'You'd better find out [about them], Paterno.'"

Onkotz couldn't have known it, but Paterno was contemplating the same thing. That week, readying for the game at Miami, an 11-point favorite, the coach started to give defenders Onkotz, Jim Kates, Steve Smear, and Neil Smith more reps in practice. Rather than show his hand that early, possibly creating a schism on his team, he explained to his players that it was going to be hot in Miami on Saturday night and that the Nittany Lions were going to need more depth.

Penn State would be flying out of Pittsburgh instead of Harrisburg for the Miami game, and Paterno, ever mindful of what he saw as the absolute necessity of rest the night before a game, took the team there on Friday. They worked out at Moon Township High, stayed in an air-conditioned hotel, took an air-conditioned bus to the air-conditioned airport and boarded an air-conditioned plane. In Miami, it was more of the same air-cooled existence. Penn State never really got to experience the heat—it would be 80 and humid at game time—until the players took the Orange Bowl field. "It worked," Paterno said. "Nobody knew how hot it was."

That kind of thoroughness would become a hallmark of Paterno's career. Nothing would go unconsidered. In the technology-drenched 21st century there can be few secrets in college football, but Paterno would still go to great lengths to shroud his program and his practices. The Grand Experiment was nice, but this was war. General George S. Patton was one of his idols, and while it was difficult to imagine Paterno slapping a player or brandishing ivory-handled pistols, he was every bit the general in terms of preparedness and tactics.

The concern about Miami's heat paid off. In what would later be seen as one of the most significant victories of the Paterno era, Penn State won 17–9. "If we'd lost that game," he said, "I probably would have told some people here to start looking around for a new coach."

The offense, with Charlie Pittman filling in superbly for Bob Campbell and with Ted Kwalick catching nine passes, was good enough. But the defense was sensational, holding the Hurricanes to just 69 yards rushing. The sophomores contributed enormously. Steve Smear played at one end. Jim Kates replaced senior Jim Zelinsky at linebacker early. Dennis Onkotz and Pete Johnson joined him there. Neil Smith went in for safety Ed Zubaty. Midway through the second quarter, there were six sophomores playing defense.

Despite the encouraging win, though, there would be more serious tests of Paterno's new leadership. As the team awaited its flight home, the coach saw two players drinking beer at the Miami airport bar. That was a violation of team policy, and the coach immediately booted one man off the team and suspended the other for two games.

Knowing how hot and nearly dehydrated the players had been the previous night, and how unhappy they were with Paterno's action, co-captain Bill Lenkaitis and quarterback Sherman asked for a meeting with the coach on Monday. At the session in his office, they suggested he might have overreacted.

Paterno listened, assembled the team, told them what he'd heard from their emissaries, and announced that since all of them knew the rules, anyone who didn't want to follow them could leave. No one did. A hurdle had been cleared, a mutiny quelled, and in a larger sense, the Rubicon had been crossed.

A week later, the Nittany Lions lost a well-played Beaver Stadium rematch with third-ranked UCLA 17–15. And then, as if some unknown power had grown weary of watching the coach's torment and flicked a switch, a light went on in State College.

The youngsters continued to grow. The 4-4-3 took root. The tension eased between coach and players. Suddenly the message was heard. The system was working. Just how well it would work only the giddiest Happy Valley optimist could have envisioned.

Penn State would not lose again for nearly three full years—1,086 days, 31 games. Before the unbeaten streak ended, Joe Paterno and Penn State would occupy the top shelf of college football.

As if through some miracle of transubstantiation, Penn State would morph into a program that was part of the national football conversation, one that consistently occupied the upper reaches of the polls. Players like Lydell Mitchell, Franco Harris, Mike Reid, and Jack Ham became All-Americans and outstanding pros. Their celebrity attracted more talent to State College. And their coach, so insecure and unsuccessful a short while ago that he had contemplated quitting, was on his way to becoming a national icon.

• • •

With an 8–2 record in 1967, Penn State earned Paterno's first postseason bid, a matchup with Florida State in the Gator Bowl. In the long interim between the regular-season-ending rout of Pitt on November 25 and the December 30 bowl in Jacksonville, Paterno learned at least one more important lesson.

Glenn Killinger, a Penn State All-American in the early 1920s and later a successful coach at West Chester (Pennsylvania) State College, was in State College watching the younger man work out his team. The sessions were hard and long as Paterno, ever the tinkerer, tried some new offensive gadgets, including a V formation and another that moved Ted Kwalick into the backfield where the end could shift right and left.

"I was real proud of myself, and I asked Killy what he thought," Paterno recalled. "He said, 'Joe, you're working them too hard.' He had watched 15 minutes, and he could see that. And he was right."

When it came to his practice routines, he would frequently accelerate and then brake. This time he backed off and through the Gator Bowl's first half it seemed to have been the correct strategy. Penn State led 17–0. But then, in what for anyone who later complained about Paterno's conservative tendencies must remain an unimaginable call, he made a strategic gaffe.

Early in the third quarter, facing a fourth-and-1 at his own 15, Paterno inexplicably had Penn State go for it. The Nittany Lions came up short and, buoyed by the stop, the Seminoles charged back, eventually tying the game on a field goal with 15 seconds left.

At the time, and in the weeks and months that followed, Paterno's move was widely derided. *Sports Illustrated* termed it the "bonehead play" of the bowl season. Others were less kind. But the coach, suddenly suffused with confidence, didn't apologize. Instead, he explained that he'd told his players not to sit on the halftime lead but rather to take chances. Then when he got the opportunity to take a flier, he said, he couldn't back down. Besides, he pointed out, that was the kind of dash and daring opponents needed to know they could expect from his program.

Although it would always be done within the carefully designed framework of his football philosophy, Penn State soon earned a reputation for gambling. The instances were rare but uncannily successful. "That [fourth-and-1 call] may be the best thing I ever did for Penn State football," Paterno eventually said.

In 1968, the talented young players were juniors and would be bolstered by the return of Mike Reid, who had missed the 1967 season with a knee injury, plus a new linebacker from Johnstown named Jack Ham.

Ham would become the quintessential player at a school that soon earned the nickname of Linebacker U. He had been an unspectacular defender at Bishop McCourt High School until, as a senior, he was shifted from the line to linebacker. Still, no major college was interested. Virginia Military Institute gave him a maybe, provided the 6'1" 165-pound player would spend a year enhancing his body and his football savvy at Massanutten (Virginia) Military Academy.

He did, but in addition to learning more football and nutrution, he discovered that military life wasn't for him. Steve Smear, Ham's high school teammate in Johnstown, recommended him to Penn State's coaches. Paterno loved what he'd seen on film, so much so that Ham was installed at outside linebacker very soon after his arrival in State College.

Good linebackers were the keys in Paterno's new defense. And along with Dennis Onkotz and Jim Kates, Ham gave Penn State three superb ones. By the time they had all graduated, the Nittany Lions were known for producing them.

There had been others before them—W.T. "Mother" Dunn, Bob Mitinger, Dave Robinson—but now it seemed that there was a linebacker assembly line in State College. In particular, Dan Radakovich and Jerry Sandusky, the latter hired as a defensive assistant in 1969, had an eye for recruiting linebacking talent and a knack for teaching the position. Freshmen who had been tailbacks or defensive backs in high school frequently were moved to linebacker at Penn State. NFL Hall of Fame quarterback Jim Kelly, a Western Pennsylvanian, said he was recruited heavily by Penn State but demurred when he'd heard Paterno, who already had landed Jeff Hostetler and Todd Blackledge, wanted to make him a linebacker.

The essential ingredient Paterno sought there was football IQ. He wanted athletic linebackers who could make judgments and adjustments on the fly. After a while, observers began to notice that while any good linebacker could read a play and then react, Penn State's linebackers seemed able to read and react simultaneously.

Over the next three decades, Penn State would find, develop, and send to the NFL a steady stream of successful LBs, including Kurt Allerman, LaVar Arrington, Ralph Baker, Bruce Bannon, Greg Buttle, Andre Collins, Shane Conlan, Ron Crosby, John Ebersole, Keith Goganious, Jim Laslavic, Lance Mehl, Matt Millen, Rick Milot, Ed O'Neil, Scott Radecik, Brandon Short, and John Skorupan. But none, Paterno and Sandusky would say decades later, were as good as Jack Ham.

• • •

If there were lingering doubts about the direction in which Paterno's program was headed, they were erased midway through the 1968 season. The 3–0 Nittany Lions revisited UCLA, this time posting an easy 21–6 win. Back in State College, as had happened after the Ohio State win years before, the students appeared to sense the turning point the nationally televised victory represented. They took to the streets to celebrate. From then on, Penn State football would have a certain cachet on campus. Tickets to home games would become pricey and much-prized commodities there and elsewhere.

With Charlie Pittman running the ball, Ted Kwalick's old high school quarterback Chuck Burkhart throwing it to the All-American tight end, and Ham bolstering an already stellar defense, the Nittany Lions were virtually unstoppable in 1968.

Now that he had the talent, routines, and systems in place, as well as the confidence of his staff, there was no stopping Paterno. An energized confidence replaced the anxiety. He drilled his team efficiently but not harshly during the week, and then on Saturdays he unleashed the hungry Lions to tear into opponents.

Only Army, in a 28–24 homecoming loss at Beaver Stadium, came close during the regular season. The Nittany Lions won their final three games—against North Carolina State, Ohio University, and Pitt—by a combined score of 142–34. Only four of their 10 opponents managed to score in double figures, while the Nittany Lions averaged nearly 35 points a contest.

While No. 1 Ohio State and No. 2 USC met in the Rose Bowl, No. 3 Penn State accepted an Orange Bowl invitation to face Big Eight champion Kansas, the nation's sixth-ranked team.

The national focus would be squarely on the Rose Bowl and Heisman winner O.J. Simpson. Penn State, despite its lofty poll position and 10–0 record, was an interloper not yet in a category with those top two teams. After all, they were from the East, where the schools might be elite but the football certainly was not.

But on the night of January 1, 1969—the Orange Bowl had been moved to prime time three years earlier to avoid overlapping with the other New Year's Day games—Penn State had the undivided attention of the nation's football fans. Paterno intended to send a message in the game at the Orange Bowl, where 11 days later Joe Namath's New York Jets would shock the Baltimore Colts in a groundbreaking Super Bowl III. "I was determined to prove [that theory about Eastern football] was baloney," Paterno said.

Unfortunately, there wasn't a lot that would shake people's beliefs during much of the game. Although Kansas was no pushover with quarterback Bobby Douglas and running backs John Riggins and Donnie Shanklin, Penn State outgained the Jayhawks convincingly. Two Burkhart interceptions kept things close and late in the fourth quarter, the Jayhawks led 14–10.

At home in Flushing, New York, Paterno's widowed mother retreated to a bathroom, locked the door, pulled her rosary beads from her purse, and began praying that fate would intervene on her beloved son's behalf. And with just more than a minute to play, it did.

Reid sacked Douglas twice to prevent Kansas from running out the clock. Paterno then sent 10 men after the punter—a formation with the charmingly simple and direct name of "10-Go Charge." One of those 10 men tipped the kick, so with 1:16 remaining the Lions took over at midfield.

On the sideline, Paterno advised Chuck Burkhart, who rarely threw deep, to try to decoy the Jayhawks defense. Campbell would run a post pattern and if he was covered, as was likely in a prevent, the quarterback should overthrow him. Then, thinking the Lions were going for broke, Kansas likely would drop back even further on the subsequent play and Burkhart could hit Ted Kwalick on a screen underneath.

Somehow Bob Campbell got open on that first route, and Burkhart hit him in stride. "I knew I had thrown a good pass," Burkhart said. "On the other hand, they've got a prevent defense working on Bobby who doesn't exactly run a 4.4 40."

Just as the press-box announcer was revealing that Kansas' Donnie Shanklin had been named the game's MVP, Penn State had a first down on the Jayhawks' 3-yard line. As it typically did, Kansas sent in an extra linebacker, Rick Abernethy, for its goal-line defense. What no one noticed until four plays later, however, was that when Abernethy entered the field, no Kansas player exited.

Tom Cherry ran twice into the 12-man defense for little gain. On third down, Paterno called the "scissors" play, in which the quarterback was supposed to fake a handoff to Pittman and give the ball to Campbell on a reverse. Incredibly, the extra player had not yet been detected, and the Jayhawks punctured the disadvantaged line easily. Not wanting to risk a handoff, Burkhart held the ball. As the clock turned to all zeroes, Burkhart scampered untouched around the left end to move Penn State to within a point at 14–13.

Remembering the hollow feeling the previous year's Gator Bowl tie had left, Paterno immediately signaled for a two-point try on what would be the game's final play.

By now, Penn State assistants in the press box had recognized Kansas' illegal advantage, even if the Jayhawks staff and the officials had not. But in the last-gasp chaos, as Paterno tried to determine the correct conversion play and Kansas coach Pepper Rodgers decided to keep the same defenders on the field, fans on both sides of the field screamed in anticipation and several shouted pleas about the 12th man went unheard.

Paterno called for a pass to Kwalick. Burkhart took the snap, but his throw was batted away. The entire Kansas team and its fans swarmed the field. This time, though, umpire Foster Grose had counted the defenders. He threw a yellow flag that Paterno would later describe as a "heaven-sent flame."

The Kansas celebration halted, the field cleared, and Penn State lined up again. This time Charlie Zapiec blocked the

Jayhawks' All-American end John Zook, and Campbell ran behind him and into end zone. Penn State had a riveting 15–14 victory.

Afterward, Grose told reporters that he was just doing his job, that he'd counted the defense before every play. It wouldn't be until a few days later, when Penn State coaches were reviewing the film, that they noticed the Jayhawks had employed 12 players for the three previous plays, as well.

The late-night lightning at the Orange Bowl electrified a national television audience. The bespectacled coach with the squeaky voice who was interviewed afterward became a familiar figure. "This Orange Bowl game put us on the map," Paterno said. But they were not yet situated in one of its most prominent locales.

Unbeaten Ohio State had defeated USC and won the No. 1 ranking in both the Associated Press and United Press International polls. USC was No. 2 in UPI, while Penn State was No. 2 in the AP voting. "The sportswriters and sportscasters heaped all kinds of praise on us but couldn't quite bring themselves to credit us—or any college in the East—with having a great football team," Paterno said. "The 'experts' couldn't get their eyes off the Big Ten, the Big Eight, the Southwest Conference, the Southeast Conference, and the Pac-10."

That attitude would reinforce Paterno's belief that the East would benefit from a major sports conference of its own, a concept he would revisit with mixed results much later. It also motivated him for a 1969 season, one that for him would end with another unbeaten record, another Orange Bowl victory, and another snub.

• • •

When Paterno and his Nittany Lions got back to Pennsylvania that January 2, the university staged a Rec Hall rally. The players were introduced to a crowd of 5,000 students, and names like Kwalick, Pittman, and Reid drew great ovations. But in the most vivid indication yet that he was now the face of Penn State football, the most thunderous roar erupted when Paterno, accompanied by university president Eric Walker, took the stage. "Every dream I've ever had," Paterno told the gathering, "has been fulfilled this season."

The hyperbole was understandable following an undefeated season and a dramatic victory in his first major bowl. But no one doubted that he had at least one more unfulfilled dream—a national championship. And with 10 returning starters on defense and sophomores like Lydell Mitchell and Franco Harris ready to supplement an offense that had averaged 35 points a game, Paterno felt his team could win one in 1969.

Viewed in another context, his words at the rally could also have had a different meaning. If his Penn State dreams were in fact fully realized, then perhaps they were a signal that he was thinking of moving on to another dream, another challenge. Perhaps his comment was a veiled valedictory message. Though few knew it at the time, he was, at that very moment, weighing a tempting offer from the NFL.

While Paterno's Nittany Lions had gone 11–0, another Pennsylvania football team was not nearly so successful in 1968. The NFL's Pittsburgh Steelers went 2–11–1 and after the season fired Coach Bill Austin. Dan Rooney, the son of the Steelers owner, knew Paterno from the coach's frequent recruiting trips to his city and its talent-rich suburbs, so he contacted the Penn State coach to gauge his interest in succeeding Austin.

The job appealed to Paterno. He liked the Rooneys. Their franchise had nowhere to go but up. The money would be sweeter. The challenge would be fresher. And in terms of Pennsylvania, he had always tilted toward Pittsburgh and away from Philadelphia. After nearly two decades in State College, Paterno had learned to appreciate Central Pennsylvania and its people. Pittsburgh, he knew, wouldn't be too drastic a change for him and his family.

Rooney and Paterno had a few more discussions about the job in the days after the Orange Bowl. The coach, eager to give the offer some serious thought, embarked on a recruiting trip alone, then flew to Los Angeles, where the 1969 NCAA convention was being held. While there, after discussing the situation with Tarman, brother George, one or two of his favorite sportswriters, and other friends and colleagues, the coach appeared ready to depart for the Steel City.

What apparently changed his mind was a phone call to Sue. Raised in one Pennsylvania small town, content to live and rear her family in another, Paterno's wife reacted to her husband's news with tears. As it would several years later when the Patriots were doing the tempting, Sue's reaction helped change Paterno's mind.

It's typically the coach's loyalty, steadfastness, and sense of perspective that are mentioned whenever the discussion turns to the many NFL jobs Paterno turned down to remain at Penn State. Perhaps it would be more accurate to credit Sue Paterno. If not for her devotion to State College and her husband's devotion to her, the Paterno legend—if one existed at all—would almost certainly be a far different one. Gone would be his reformer's cape, his idealist's sword, the notion that what was important in his profession were the lives it changed. What would have replaced those things were the big cash and cold statistics that are the measures of pro sports success. Few in the NFL want to hear about Camus or Virgil, and the only reform that matters there are changes in the game's basic agreement.

The following day, Paterno issued a press release informing the public that he would be staying at Penn State. Its wording implied a far different reality than his "every dream fulfilled" speech a week earlier, which was further evidence that he indeed had been on the doorstep of departure. "To leave Penn State at this time would be to leave with the feeling of a job undone and a great challenge still unfulfilled," the statement said. In a matter of a few days, Paterno had discovered a new unfulfilled dream.

Coincidentally, Sue Paterno, whose hometown of Latrobe was not far from Pittsburgh, had been to one pro football game in her life, and it was in Pittsburgh. The drunks and foul language had turned her off, which may also explain why her husband never seriously considered any of the offers the Philadelphia Eagles would make. She would say later that she broke down on the phone that night because she felt her husband was not being fair to himself, that he would have been walking away from Penn State for reasons opposed to his Grand Experiment rhetoric.

"He'd waited all his life for this job. Why would he suddenly chuck it?" she said. "He wanted to make Penn State a unique spot.... Also, there was his feeling toward this group of kids who were his first complete team. He'd become very attached to them."

8

THE BOND BETWEEN JOE PATERNO and his "first complete team" was anticipation. It would have been difficult for Paterno to walk away from that talented 1969 team. Not only had most of its players been recruited on his watch, but the team was riding a 19-game unbeaten streak. Ted Kwalick was gone, but virtually every other key player returned, including all but one starting defender. And on offense, senior running back Charlie Pittman would be supplemented by sophomores Lydell Mitchell and Franco Harris.

They began the season ranked No. 2 behind Ohio State and stayed there until a half-hearted effort in a 17–14 win at Kansas State dropped them to No. 5. Except for a 15–14 comeback win against Syracuse on October 18, the Nittany Lions were never seriously challenged for the remainder of the regular season, rolling up an average of 31 points a game and allowing just 8. They were 10–0 and ranked third. Dennis Onkotz, Mike Reid, Neil Smith, and Pittman would be named first-team All-Americans, and Reid would win the Outland Trophy as the nation's best interior lineman.

They were headed for another New Year's bowl, but selecting one would not be easy. Independents like Penn State—or those from conferences not affiliated with any bowl—had to make their decisions during the third week of November.

At that point, there remained four major unbeatens—Ohio State, Texas, Penn State, and Arkansas. Penn State still had regular-season games left with Pitt and North Carolina. Texas still had to play Texas A&M and Arkansas, while the Razorbacks had Texas Tech and Texas.

As the defending champion, Ohio State had a firm grip on the top spot in the polls. But the Big Ten was locked into the Rose Bowl, and conference rules stipulated that no team could play in two consecutively. Ohio State, the Rose Bowl winner the previous January, was prohibited from returning there or going to any other bowl, for that matter.

Since Paterno and virtually everyone else assumed the Buckeyes would beat Michigan in their finale, earn a second consecutive Big Ten title, and finish as the unbeaten top-ranked team, there would be no chance for a head-to-head meeting between Ohio State and any of the other contenders.

Texas and Arkansas, meanwhile, were due to play each other on December 6 in a game that would determine the Cotton Bowl's host. Penn State could opt to play the winner in the Cotton Bowl, or it could return to the Orange Bowl.

Paterno allowed the players to vote. But before he did, for at least two good reasons, he wanted to get the opinions of the black players on his roster. Both bowls would take place in the South, a region still adjusting, often painfully, to new civil rights legislation. Secondly, in part because there were so few blacks in the student body or on the faculty and because of the school's rural surroundings, Penn State was having difficulty increasing the number of black recruits. Paterno didn't need to be seen as racially insensitive.

Joe Paterno clutches the Lambert Trophy in New York on December 6, 1973, after it was awarded to his team as emblematic of collegiate gridiron supremacy in the east. (AP PHOTO/DAVE PICKOFF)

Opposing Sugar Bowl coach Paul "Bear" Bryant of Alabama (left) shares a smile with Joe Paterno as they met for a press conference in New Orleans, on December 28, 1978. (AP PHOTO)

Joe Paterno waves as he gets a victory ride in the Louisiana Superdome Saturday night after his Nittany Lions beat Georgia 27–23 in the Sugar Bowl in New Orleans, Louisiana, on January 1, 1983. (AP PHOTO/BILL FEIG)

Joe and Suzanne Paterno arrive for a state dinner at the White House on Tuesday, March 31, 1987, in Washington, D.C. The dinner was in honor of Prime Minister and Mrs. Chirac of France. (AP PHOTO/DENNIS COOK)

Joe Paterno (right) and Stanford University coach Bill Walsh talk before their football teams meet in the Blockbuster Bowl in Miami, Florida, on January 2, 1993. (AP PHOTO/PHIL COALE)

Penn State players dump ice water on head coach Joe Paterno after Penn State defeated Texas 38–15 at the Fiesta Bowl in Tempe, Arizona, on January 1, 1997. (AP PHOTO/JEFF ROBBINS)

Joe Paterno watches their college football game against Coastal Carolina from the sideline with his three quarterbacks, Daryll Clark (left), Paul Cianciolo (second from right), and Pat Devlin (right) on Saturday, August 30, 2008, at Beaver Stadium. After No. 22 Penn State routed Coastal Carolina 66–10, Paterno tied Florida State's Bobby Bowden atop the career wins list for major college coaches at 373 victories. (AP PHOTO/CAROLYN KASTER)

Hall of Fame coach Joe Paterno laughs as he answers a question at his weekly NCAA college football news conference on Tuesday, August 31, 2010, in State College, Pennsylvania. (AP PHOTO/PAT LITTLE)

The Nittany Lions' trip to Miami the previous year had been pleasant and uneventful. The assassination of President John F. Kennedy in Dallas just six years earlier was still fresh in their minds, so the black athletes opted for Miami and the Orange Bowl.

Paterno informed the rest of the team of their decision. He also explained the pros and cons of the two bowls from his perspective. It looked increasingly like Ohio State, the defending national champ, would be No. 1 again entering the bowl season. All the unbeaten Buckeyes had to do was beat 7–2 Michigan on November 22. If that happened, their no-bowl season complete, they'd be sitting at No. 1. In that scenario, either team Penn State faced in the Cotton Bowl would be No. 2 at best. The Orange Bowl? Well, it was hard to knock a trip to Miami in winter.

Though a lot remained unprocessed, the Nittany Lions not surprisingly voted to return to sunny Miami and face Big Eight champion and sixth-ranked Missouri in the Orange Bowl.

"We all had a good time there the year before," Onkotz said. "There was no way we could have known it then, of course, but it turned out to be a big mistake. That was the last time Joe let his team pick which bowl they were going to."

On November 22, the sixth anniversary of the Kennedy assassination, Michigan ruined their plans. The Wolverines, who were going to the Rose Bowl win or lose, upset the Buckeyes. Ironically, Michigan's first-year coach, Bo Schembechler, had been hired the previous off-season only after Paterno turned down a chance to coach there.

Texas now assumed the No. 1 spot in the polls and Arkansas was No. 2, setting up a showdown that after both won their next-to-last games came to be labeled the "Big Shootout." Penn State victories in its final two games changed nothing. They were No. 3.

Paterno and his team had miscalculated. The idea that the December 6 matchup in Fayetteville, Arkansas, would crown the national champ gained currency with each passing day. ABC began to tout Texas-Arkansas as a battle for final supremacy. And so did former Oklahoma coach Bud Wilkinson, now an ABC commentator.

Worst of all from Paterno's perspective was the role played by President Nixon, a backup lineman at Whittier College decades earlier and a football fanatic.

People like Wilkinson, a prominent Republican, had been attempting to get the president to attend a college football game to commemorate the sport's 100th anniversary. When the significance of the Texas-Arkansas game became clear, White House chief of staff H.R. Haldeman sent a memo to his boss urging him to take advantage of these "great circumstances." On December 1, Nixon announced that he would fly in for the game, lending it even more heft.

Before the game and before the season's final polls, Nixon also made it known that he'd be presenting a plaque to the Texas-Arkansas winner, honoring it as the national champion of 1969. The president, in effect, had pre-empted the rest of the season and the final polls.

In retrospect, it's clear that the two decisions were minor prongs in Nixon's Southern Strategy—the Republican's plan to permanently push the traditionally Democratic South into the GOP's column.

Whatever the reasoning, Paterno and Penn State backers fumed. When Republican Pennsylvania governor Raymond Shafer griped and the White House got more than 90,000 complaining calls, telegrams, and letters, Nixon sought to douse the political fires. Press secretary Ron Ziegler soon announced that his boss planned to present Paterno with a second plaque, this one honoring Penn State for its national-best, 29-game unbeaten streak.

When a White House representative phoned the coach to ask him to come to Washington for a plaque presentation ceremony, the angry Paterno told him to tell the President "he could shove it." Publicly, he was more tactful, issuing a statement said that his team "would be disappointed at this time...to receive anything other than a plaque for the number-one team."

Texas beat Arkansas 15–14, and afterward Nixon visited the Longhorns locker room. As promised, he presented Coach Darrell Royal with the unofficial championship award. "In presenting this plaque," Nixon said, "I want to say first that the AP and the UPI will name Texas No. 1, as we know, after this game."

Now there seemed no way the Nittany Lions could be voted No. 1 if they and Texas both won on New Year's. Columnists outside the east treated the final voting as a *fait accompli*, noting that Penn State was paying the price for its weak schedule and its decision to go to Miami—even though at the time it couldn't possibly have known the Cotton Bowl host would be the nation's top team.

"Who has Texas or Arkansas played?" asked Paterno in response, his normal circumspection in discussing such matters gone. "How many intersectional games has the Southwest Conference won? Five? Six?"

Penn State would defeat Missouri in a defensive-minded Orange Bowl 10–3, a result that was unlikely to persuade many poll voters to flip-flop the two top teams, especially since earlier that day Texas had edged Notre Dame 21–17.

Though his was a lost cause, Paterno felt compelled after the bowl victory to lobby one more time for his undefeated team since the AP had withheld its last rankings until the bowl games were done due to the controversy.

"I don't like to keep pushing this thing," Paterno said after the Orange Bowl victory, during which his defense had intercepted a bowl-record seven passes, "but I still think we have as much right to No. 1 as Texas or anybody else. Why should I sit back and let the President of the United States say that so-and-so is number one when I've got 50 kids who've worked their tails off for me for three years?"

It was too little too late. A day later, the AP confirmed UPI's earlier decision. Texas was No. 1. Penn State was No. 2.

The painful episode stung Paterno for a long time. In his autobiography, written 20 years later, the wound was still fresh. "The bloodcurdling nerve!" Paterno wrote. "Nixon *favored* us with an honor that any idiot consulting the record book could see that we had taken for ourselves, thank you, without his help."

Actually, the snub appeared to bother Paterno more than it did some of his players.

"It really wasn't that big a deal," Dennis Onkotz said. "The media wasn't nearly as big back then, so you didn't hear about it all the time the way you would now. And to be honest, we were all so busy. I was a biophysics major, so I had a lot of classes that took a lot of time and work. I didn't have a lot of time to think about who was number one."

Curiously, the incident—which, thanks to the identity of its principals, generated enormous news coverage for the time—may have helped Paterno and Penn State by raising the national profile of each. Though the coach was viewed as a crybaby in Texas, Arkansas, and elsewhere in the South, others saw his as another principled stand, a connection his supporters made sure to note.

"I think that [controversy] differentiated Paterno from if not all then just about all of the coaches in the country," said Ed Junker, the president of Penn State's board of trustees, to academic Nicholas Evan Sarantakes for a 2006 article on the affair. "It's trite to say it, but it definitely made him a living legend as far as Penn State is concerned."

Sarantakes himself said that after studying the matter carefully, it was his opinion that it all worked to the coach's advantage, "bringing more attention to a football program on the rise." Paterno eventually would agree, saying much later that "those two Orange Bowls made our program."

They also made Paterno a lifelong advocate of a playoff system. The fact that coaches—who in many cases ceded their responsibility to sports information directors—and sportswriters were responsible for the crowning of a champion seemed illogical. You work and sweat and grimace for an entire year, and then you leave the ultimate decision to a bunch of people who might never have seen your team play? What kind of system was that?

In some years it worked. But in others—1969 being an infamous example—it resulted in chaos and controversy. "There was no way of anybody being satisfied," Paterno said. "With a little planning, [a playoff system] would not be hard to accomplish. But everybody knows how some people in power tremble over the prospect of change."

His desire for playoffs, like his unhappiness over how it all turned out in 1969, never vanished. When Penn State students invited him to give the school's commencement address in 1973, he found that forum a fitting place to raise the issue again.

It was June 16, 1973, one day short of the first anniversary of the break-in at the Watergate complex in Washington, D.C., that would trigger a nation-shaking scandal.

"I'd like to know," he said with the obvious delight of a speaker who knew he was about to deliver a bring-down-the-house line, "how could a president know so little about Watergate in 1973 and so much about college football in 1969?"

9

THE OFFICIAL CANONIZATION OF ST. JOE took place in
1973. As a morally confused nation slipped out of Vietnam and
stepped into Watergate, Paterno would earn his halo and ascend
to the mountaintop of American heroes. Curiously, he would do
so away from the football field, even though his Nittany Lions
would go 12–0 that season.

The three events that marked his *annus mirabilis* seem almost
Biblical—a great temptation, a sermon on Mount Nittany, and
a tearful, spiritual awakening in the heart of Babel.

Before 1973 was over, St. Joe would overshadow Paterno the
coach. Thanks to the events of January 5, June 16, and December
13, his name and face would become symbols of steadfast virtue,
not only in sports but in the rapidly changing world beyond.
Paterno's actions, words, and tears helped to counter a cynicism
created by a self-destructing president, soaring oil prices, gasoline
shortages, movie antiheroes, and baseball's designated hitter.

Penn State's ultimate football success, when it came a decade
later, would enhance his image and lay to rest whatever doubts
remained about his abilities as a coach, a recruiter, and a leader.
But football alone would no longer define him. From 1973 on,
the first items on his resume would always be the virtues he

showcased that year. They would be implanted so deeply in the public consciousness that they would endure no matter how many games he lost in the decades to come, no matter how many of his players got in trouble, and no matter how irritable or curmudgeonly he became.

• • •

On January 5, at a news conference in Rec Hall, Paterno announced that he was not leaving Penn State, ending both weeks of speculation and the single most transformative episode in his long career at the school.

It had begun innocently seven weeks earlier in Chestnut Hill, Massachusetts. On November 18, 1972, Penn State defeated Boston College 45–26 for its ninth consecutive victory. As Paterno exited the Alumni Stadium field, well-wishers surrounded him. One was New England Patriots owner Billy Sullivan. The blunt and good-natured Irishman shook the Penn State coach's hand and then, eschewing any small talk, asked him if he'd be interested in coaching his team.

His team, an original American Football League member for which Sullivan had paid $25,000 in 1959, needed help. Thirteen years old, having gone through the AFL's merger with the NFL and a recent change in its geographical surname from Boston to New England, the Patriots still had not won a championship.

In 1971, general manager Upton Bell, the son of the NFL's first commissioner, had wanted to replace Coach John Mazur with Paterno. Sullivan had hesitated then. Now, with Bell gone and the Pats headed toward a 3–11 finish, he could wait no longer.

A public-relations professional by trade, Sullivan saw in the Penn State coach an easy sell. From Sullivan's perspective, the hiring would make good football and business sense. Though

Paterno was the hottest coach in the college game, he was more than his record. His Ivy League background, his straightforward nature, his reputation as a reformer, and his intellectual bent all made him unique and extremely attractive to New Englanders.

Sullivan knew the Steelers and other NFL clubs had tried to lure Paterno in the past and failed. Somehow he was going to have to turn the coach's head.

With details of the just-completed game still swimming in his head, Paterno was polite but noncommittal with Sullivan at Boston College. A job change, he told the owner, wasn't something he could get his head around at that moment. But he promised to consider it.

The following Friday, as Paterno readied for bed and the next day's season finale with Pitt, Sullivan phoned him at home. "Joe," he said, "what if you not only coach my team but own a piece of it, as well?"

For Paterno, who had been courted before and would be again, the affair suddenly took on a whole new glow.

Just days after the Nittany Lions' 9–2 regular season ended with a 49–27 drubbing of Pitt, Paterno flew to New York to talk details with Sullivan. In addition to making him a minority owner in an NFL franchise, the four-year deal had a starting salary of $200,000, with guaranteed annual increases of at least $25,000. He would get two cars and between 3 and 6 percent of the team.

Ownership aside, the total compensation topped $1.4 million, a staggering sum for a man making $30,000 a year; and it was a figure no coach, college or pro, had yet reached.

Paterno was floored. He was making a good but by no means extravagant salary. His fifth child, Scott, had been born a few weeks earlier. He had no stock, no bonds, and little savings. Now there could be money for private schools for the kids, money for nice vacations, money for a large home in a leafy Boston suburb or on Beacon Hill—and, most intriguingly, money for a summer house on Cape Cod.

Thinking about that last item took him back to his days at Brown where he'd always felt like an outsider. His classmates, or so it seemed to the kid from Brooklyn, lived in a closed universe, one unattainable to a skinny Italian kid who wore white sweaters to fraternity parties. "There was no question," he said of his undergraduate experience in Providence, "[that] as a swarthy kid from Brooklyn, I was different."

If there was one symbol of that difference, one thing all of his antagonists appeared to have in common, it was a summer house on Cape Cod. "[It was something] every rich Yankee kid I'd met at Brown assumed was coming to him, the same as inheriting his dad's club membership."

Now he could enter their circle. He could have one, too. Paterno was intoxicated by the promise of delayed retribution, by the allure of a place on that 65-mile, hook-shaped sliver of sand, which was long a Brahmin retreat.

Intellectually, he knew he was bucking his own beliefs. How many times, after all, had he spoken out about the dangers of a desire for material things?

"A lot of people in this world are driving themselves nuts because of advertising—you know, the good life, the beautiful girl and the beautiful guy sailing down the river, all that kind of junk," Paterno once said. "I think we've built up a world of make-believe that really tantalizes people. I've never let that bother me.... My kids can swim just as well in a community pool as they can in a private pool."

But apparently being able to swim in the Atlantic Ocean in front of your own vacation house was another matter. He and his family would be right there, alongside all those Brown classmates who went on to lucrative careers in Boston law firms or in Wall Street investment banks.

Paterno told Sullivan he'd give him an answer soon after his No. 5-ranked Nittany Lions played No. 2 Oklahoma in the December 31 Sugar Bowl. "But I really wanted it," Paterno said.

The negotiations had remained private as Paterno readied Penn State—a 13½-point underdog—for the Sooners. But not long before he flew to New Orleans on December 26, a Patriots board member, upset by the size of the proposed contract, leaked word to the *Boston Globe*. Sportswriter Bob Ryan was dispatched to Louisiana with Paterno his sole focus.

The whispers had reached New Orleans by the time Paterno's plane landed. Soon the rumors made it to State College, where concerned university administrators sent Robert Patterson, vice president for finance and operations, to New Orleans on a mission of his own—to lock up Paterno with a long-term contract.

"I had come to Penn State in 1967, and during that time football had become so successful that it became clear that it was going to be an integral part of the university and its growth," Patterson said. "And Joe Paterno was a key part of that. We had heard these rumors about the Patriots, and we decided that the time had come to get him a contract."

The coach had worked year to year without any formal agreement, secure in his status as a tenured professor in the College of Liberal Arts. If everyone else at the university got a raise, he got one, too.

His situation was unusual and increasingly out of step in a college sports world that was shedding its ivied past and becoming more like a business—a big business. In 1968, Paterno had shocked Alabama's Bear Bryant with the modest details of his salary and benefits.

Bryant told Paterno he was underpaid. The university, he noted, was benefitting enormously from its football program. Paterno ought to be compensated accordingly. "Your contract ought to be for five years," Bryant advised, "and you ought to be able to roll it over. You ought to have a car, and you ought to have a country club. You ought to have 200 tickets—season tickets."

Paterno and Sullivan met in New Orleans at a hotel near the French Quarter where Penn State's most powerful alumni were staying. The coach also had discussions with Robert Patterson.

Normally in the days before a big game—any game, for that matter—Paterno wouldn't have tolerated any kind of disruption in routine or focus. That he was willing to involve himself in such a major distraction while preparing for the Sugar Bowl indicated just how seriously he took Sullivan's offer.

During a Sugar Bowl dinner at New Orleans' famed Antoine's, Ryan spotted Sullivan greeting Paterno. He wrote about the encounter, and the speculation intensified.

Whether or not the distractions were the reason, Penn State played poorly. With star running back John Cappelletti sidelined by a stomach flu, Oklahoma limited the Nittany Lions to just 49 yards of offense. The Sooners won 14–0, and it could have been much worse.

The *Globe* published a January 2 story stating that the two men were continuing to negotiate and that differences over the size of Paterno's ownership stake were all that prevented a deal from being completed.

Soon everyone had a theory about what was going to happen. One Pennsylvania columnist suggested that a sticking point might be the fact that Paterno would become eligible for a half-salary pension in 1975 after 25 years at Penn State—as if $15,000 a year were going to impact a deal of this size. Others suggested that the two NFL jobs in New York were the only ones that interested him—he could either succeed Ewbank with the Jets, or he could join the Giants, his favorite pro team when he was growing up in Brooklyn.

On New Year's Day 1973, Penn State's traveling party returned to State College, but the negotiating didn't end. Later that week Paterno met with new Pats GM Bucko Kilroy in a New Jersey Holiday Inn. He also had at least six discussions with Patterson.

Though that's exactly how things played out, the coach has always insisted he wasn't trying to leverage the Pats' offer into a richer Penn State contract. "Obviously, I was very pleased they wanted to give me a new contract," Paterno said. "But it was a very, very difficult decision."

State College slid into a panic over the possibility of losing its best-known citizen. The university had never enjoyed such a lofty national reputation, and its staff and the residents of the town were proud of it. A local magazine, *Town & Gown*, launched an organized effort to keep him. More than 19,000 postcards were mailed, urging Paterno to stay. The hurriedly revamped January edition of the magazine had the coach's photo on its cover alongside a bold-faced plea, "Joe: Don't Go Pro!" Similarly themed bumper stickers also appeared.

"We just felt we had a vehicle that could help influence him to stay," said *Town & Gown* publisher Mimi Barash Coopersmith, a Penn State grad and later a university trustee. "It was a voice for the community to respond, and they did."

There was little question that Paterno was leaning toward New England. On Thursday, January 4, Sullivan phoned sports columnist Dick Young of the *New York Daily News* and leaked the news that Penn State's coach planned to accept the job. Paterno, Young wrote, would fly to New York on Friday where, in a Plaza Hotel suite, he and Sullivan would finalize the deal.

Meanwhile, on Thursday night in State College, Sue Paterno invited their closest friends, sports information director Tarman and his wife, Louise, to their house for cocktails and dinner. Paterno informed his friends that he was going to the NFL and that he wanted Tarman to come along as an aide.

The two couples discussed the possibilities of the NFL and life in Boston, as well as how difficult it would be for them to leave State College. Finally, Paterno offered a champagne toast to their good fortune. He would later characterize the evening as "the most cheerless celebration party I'd ever been at."

After the Tarmans left, the coach sensed that his wife's unease was worsening. She'd known since the beginning. Not long after his New York meeting with Sullivan, he'd told her the offer was so lucrative that "I had to take it." She had seemed, if not upbeat, at least open-minded about a move. But as a final decision neared, Paterno said, it became clear "she wasn't crazy about it."

She had opposed his taking the Steelers job several years earlier, and now she was having second thoughts about New England. Once again, hers would be the opinion that most influenced the outcome.

Although he then seemed certain to take the Pats job, the meticulously prepared Paterno had made backup plans. He'd asked Patterson to reserve the university's jet for a flight early Friday. In that scenario, he and Patterson would fly to Pittsburgh where they would discuss a new Penn State contract with lawyer Chuck Queenan, who had represented Steelers quarterback Terry Bradshaw.

The Paternos stayed up talking until 3:00 AM, at which time the coach was so convinced he was NFL bound that he called Patterson and told him to cancel the Pittsburgh flight. He'd be flying instead to New York.

Before they turned off the bedroom light, Paterno joked with his wife that this would be the first time she'd ever slept with a millionaire. Sue Paterno didn't laugh.

He tossed and turned in bed, and after a few hours he arose. He later termed it "the night I was forced to decide who I am." His wife awoke at 5:30 and asked him why he wasn't getting dressed. He told her he'd changed his mind. "I'm not going."

Paterno telephoned Sullivan with the news, thanking him for the generous offer. "God bless you, Joe," said the disappointed owner, who soon afterward hired the coach whose team beat Paterno's in the Sugar Bowl, Oklahoma's Chuck Fairbanks.

At about 7:30 AM, Paterno notified Tarman. He then called a relieved Patterson with the news and asked him to reschedule the Pittsburgh flight. Patterson tracked down the pilots. After his earlier call, they'd gotten drunk and, according to FAA regulations, needed 12 hours before they could fly again. "I told them I didn't care how they did it," Patterson remembered, "but I wanted that goddamned plane ready to leave in an hour."

They made the flight, and in Queenan's office Paterno signed a new five-year deal with Penn State that hiked his salary to an estimated $100,000 a year. The details were never made public, a habit Paterno would continue for the rest of his career. When the coach said he also wanted more life insurance, a physical with a Pittsburgh doctor was hastily arranged. Despite the stresses of the past few weeks, he passed.

Meanwhile, Tarman, who had been besieged with questions about the coach's status for days, planned a news conference for 10:00 AM Saturday in Rec Hall. Most of the sportswriters contacted assumed it would be a farewell to Paterno. Instead the coach waved his new Penn State contract for emphasis and informed them he'd be staying. And barring some "drastic" change, he'd be there for the remainder of his career.

When asked about his rationale for turning down so much money, Paterno cited *The Aeneid* and one of the many life lessons it taught him. "When you choose wrong, as Aeneas found out, life comes down on you with some terrible whacks," Paterno said.

• • •

Virtually overnight Paterno became a national hero. Money was being discussed more than ever in sports. And while free agency hadn't yet burst onto the scene, the notion that a coach could be offered $1.4 million was stunning; that he had turned it down was unthinkable.

Both sides in what remained of the 1960s culture war adopted the coach as a hero. To the right, his decision to remain an educator at a small-town college was a reaffirmation of their values. To the left, he had turned away from material gain and the blandishments of a powerful establishment institution.

Those in the media who were not yet on Paterno's bandwagon leaped aboard. Here was a noble figure, a great coach with great values, an admirable hybrid of Vince Lombardi and Albert Schweitzer.

Suddenly the coaching profession, the entire sports world, had its *beau idéal*. While the Grand Experiment had been high-minded philosophy, Paterno proved his principles extended beyond the hypothetical, beyond his rhetoric.

In the future, all coaches and their programs would be measured against Paterno and Penn State. His name would become synonymous with high graduation rates, "student-athletes," the dangers of excess, and doing things the right way.

Sports Illustrated's William Johnson would write soon afterward that Paterno "did not believe that money is the root of all the fruits of life…. In these days when feet of clay and souls of brass seem to be the identifying marks of so many leaders, the mere fact that Joe Paterno expresses himself with an unforked tongue is apparently enough to warrant standing ovations and hero worship."

At a time when most successful football coaches typically fell into a few stereotypical categories—militaristic (Woody Hayes), shrewd and shady (Bear Bryant), or obsessive (Vince Lombardi), Paterno was something admirably indefinable. The closest reference point might have been John Wooden. The UCLA basketball coach, who would seek advice from Paterno when he was asked to be Purdue's commencement speaker in 1975, had a style best described as gentlemanly precise. Like Paterno, Wooden admired good grooming, fair play, and the positive principles inherent in sports. The modest Midwesterner and the brash Brooklynite were both devoted family men. Most importantly, both produced winning teams, though with 10 national titles, the UCLA mentor had the edge there. But unlike Paterno, Wooden had never been an outspoken voice of reform. And as would later become clear, while he might not have been fully aware of booster abuses in his program, Wooden had at least been willing to turn a blind eye to them.

The version of Paterno that emerged was so saintly that the coach himself couldn't compete with it. He had his flaws, as anyone who ever coached with or played for him knew. "Players who play for him understand that he is an acquired taste," running back Charlie Pittman said. His program almost certainly was purer than the vast majority, but it was not then and never would be perfect. While there's never been a hint of a major scandal there, his players got into trouble, too.

As his hometown *Centre Daily Times* felt compelled to remind readers in an editorial that first week of 1973, "[Paterno] has his critics. Those jealous; those who disagree with his philosophies; those who can't believe he's sincere in his outspoken stands; those who can't tolerate or understand his brutal frankness."

But all of that would be overwhelmed by the growing legend of St. Joe.

March 31 was declared "Joe Paterno Day" in Pennsylvania by governor Milton Shapp. That night 700 guests paid to attend a banquet in the coach's honor at the Penn Harris Motor Inn near Harrisburg. It resembled an episode of the old television show, *This Is Your Life*. He was given a new Dodge Charger and a trip to Italy. Coach Zev Graham from Brooklyn Prep was there, as were several Prep classmates and fellow Brown alums. John Oswald, the university president, also attended as did numerous politicians and Paterno relatives, including his 76-year-old mother.

"No one could be more deserving," Florence Paterno said. "Joe was always considerate. Even as a little boy, he was that way."

Paterno and Penn State unquestionably benefited from his canonization. It became much easier to convince recruits and their parents that his intentions were true. He commanded a new degree of respect. Everyone, including the 4,650 members of PSU's graduating class of 1973, wanted him as a speaker. The positive publicity the university received as the result of his decision to stay was priceless. Out-of-state applications and overall contributions increased. So did requests for season tickets. Administrators began making plans for another Beaver Stadium expansion, and by 1978 its seating capacity had grown by more than 19,000.

The coach's bespectacled face became the Penn State brand. He and Penn State were inseparable. A school that had long lacked an identity had one now. The blue blazers that the conservative-dressing Paterno favored became the unofficial uniform of administrators. The old agricultural university's creamery developed a Peachy Paterno flavor of ice cream. The student bookstore was soon bursting with Paterno-related merchandise, everything from bobbleheads to ties.

But he also found some elements of his newfound fame unsettling. When *Sports Illustrated*'s William Johnson asked Paterno if he considered himself a "folk hero," he cringed.

"I get letters from people who seem to think that if only Joe Paterno can spend 20 minutes with a kid, then his troubles will be all over," he said. "Nuts. People want to give me too much credit. I'm a football coach who has won a few games— remember?"

He would win 12 more in 1973.

• • •

Among the countless invitations that poured into Paterno's office in the first half of 1973 was one from the school's senior class asking him to be their commencement speaker. Paterno initially was reluctant to accept. He said he finally agreed to do so because of what had happened after he turned down the Patriots.

"I accepted," he said in the address, "because I realize that in a day when materialism is rampant, many of you felt that my interest in doing other things besides making money has in some way helped you to reaffirm your ideal of a life of service, of dignity, and a life of meaning which goes beyond financial success.... Money alone will not make you happy; success without honor is an unseasoned dish."

The news that Paterno would be addressing Penn State's graduates drew reporters from around the country to State College for the event on June 16, 1973. The school's students had never before asked a coach, or a sports figure of any kind, to deliver their valedictory speech. Like the journalists, parents, and friends in attendance that day, the graduates were eager to hear him.

Paterno appeared somewhat self-conscious as, capless and wearing a long academic gown with a narrow white stole, he walked to the microphone on a stage that had been constructed on familiar turf—atop Beaver Stadium's field. In front of him were more than 4,000 graduates, their relatives and guests, plus various faculty and administration members.

The Brown graduate, with the help of his English-major wife, had devoted considerable energies to his task. Not surprisingly, he sprinkled the talk with literary references, quotes from John Steinbeck, W.H. Auden, and Robert Browning. He tried to maintain a mood that was at once lighthearted and profound— razzing President Nixon with his now-famous putdown one moment and in the next advising the young men and women that "we must get better before we can get perfect."

As he knew, it was impossible to give a commencement address in June 1973 without mentioning Watergate. The U.S. would end its long and costly involvement in Vietnam that year, but the residual anger over the war had turned to cynicism during the drawn-out scandal that a year later resulted in Nixon's resignation. Paterno urged the students not to get discouraged or turn their backs on civic involvement.

"The system, the organization, the method, the government— is you. If each of us is easily seduced by expediency, by selfishness, by ambition regardless of cost to our principles, then the spectacle of Watergate will surely mark the end of this grand experiment in democracy.... [The Watergate principals] were ready to change the world. They didn't trust the over-thirty generation. I warn you—don't underestimate the world. It can overwhelm you."

He touched on the appeal and the benefits of football, as well.

"We strive to be No. 1. We work hard to achieve our goals, and when Saturday comes around and we walk on the grass in this stadium, we stand as a team. We tighten our belts. We look across at our opponents. We say, 'Come on, let's go. Let's see how good you are. Let's play.' We are ready. We play with enthusiasm and recklessness. We aren't afraid to lose. If we win, great, wonderful—and the alumni are happy for another week. But, win or lose, it is the competition that matters."

And then he directed those same lessons toward life and the futures the graduates were walking into.

"It is being involved in a common cause, which brings us joy and memories, which endure in teammates. It is making our very best effort, that we have stretched to the very limit of our ability, which makes us bigger men and more able to stretch again, to reach even higher as we undertake new challenges."

Finally, he concluded with words that were heartfelt and courageous. In an era when law-and-order fervor was beginning to crack back at 1960s permissiveness, Paterno did not ridicule or diminish the rebellious spirit that had marked this particular class of Penn State students. He applauded it.

"Let me end on a personal note. We have loved you because you have given us our challenge, our joy of living. You have inspired us to stretch. You have disrupted our comfortable thinking. You have made us reevaluate, think again about our ideal and our principles. You have made us look again at our souls.

"We hope you have loved each other because a little bit of you is inside one another. John Steinbeck said in *The Grapes of Wrath*, 'Maybe man doesn't own his own soul, only a piece of a big man.' I cannot adequately describe to you the love that permeates a good football team, a love of one another. Perhaps as one of my players said, 'We grow together in love—hating the coach.'

"But to be in a locker room before a big game and to gather a team around and to look at grown men with tears in their eyes huddling close to each other…reaching out to be a part of each other…to look into strong faces, which say, 'If we can only do it today'…to be with aggressive, ambitious people who have lost themselves in something bigger than they are—this is what living is all about.

"We have shared four years together, years we will never forget, and we hope this short journey has made us all a little better. We wish you Godspeed, and we wish you good luck. But most of all, we wish you peace."

• • •

John Cappelletti had been a defensive back and punt returner until Paterno moved the junior into the offensive backfield in 1972. Unbridled, the chiseled junior would run for 1,117 yards and 12 touchdowns as Penn State went 10–2.

As a senior a year later, bigger and stronger, he increased those totals to 1,522 yards and 17 touchdowns. He rushed for more than 100 yards eight times and surpassed the 200-yard mark three consecutive games at the end of the season, a stretch that would help him win the Heisman Trophy.

He was a bruising, punishing, physical runner, a throwback to the era when Paterno had arrived in State College. "We knock people down," said lineman Mark Markovich, "and when they get up, Cappy comes by and knocks them down again."

The 1973 defense—anchored by future NFL players Mike Hartenstine, Randy Crowder, and Greg Buttle—was the perfect complement to the run-oriented attack Paterno employed all season.

Penn State ran roughshod through what proved to be an unusually soft schedule. The Lions thrashed all 11 regular-season opponents—none ranked when they met—by an average margin of 26 points. They ran for nearly 3,000 yards (2,994). They had 10 players—seven on defense—picked in the next NFL draft.

But the Lions' timing was awful. Their six traditional rivals from the East—Pitt, West Virginia, Army, Navy, Maryland, and Syracuse—experienced off-years. Army and Navy would never again return to the level they occupied when Penn State began scheduling them. Syracuse and West Virginia were slipping, too. And the five other opponents—Stanford, 0–11 Iowa, Air Force, North Carolina State, and Ohio University—were hardly a college football murderer's row at the time.

Worse, five other teams—Alabama, Notre Dame, Oklahoma, Ohio State, and Michigan (the latter two tied each other)—also finished unbeaten that regular season. Penn State would defeat LSU in the Orange Bowl 16–9, but the win couldn't propel the Nittany Lions above the No. 5 spot in the final rankings.

Paterno's frustration with the polls mounted. What did they want? Penn State had won 62 of 68 games. It finished in the top 10 virtually every season. It produced All-Americans, NFL draftees, and in Cappelletti, a Heisman winner. They didn't cheat. They went to class. They behaved on the field.

Despite all the praise being heaped upon him and his program, when the voters had to make a choice between Penn State and Texas or Ohio State or Alabama or Oklahoma, the Nittany Lions invariably came in second. It was guilt by association. To the people who voted in the national polls, Eastern football didn't compare with the power conferences in the other regions.

One Paterno-friendly writer, Pat Putnam of *Sports Illustrated*, came to the program's defense. "More than its Eastern image, Penn State's cross is a soft schedule made up years ago under another less ambitious regime. Texas grows fat on people like Rice and TCU and Baylor," he wrote, "and it matters not. Notre Dame dines on Army, Navy, and Pitt, and it bothers no one. But let Penn State take on Ohio University, and sirens go off."

George Paterno was not as circumspect about the ongoing snubs. In his memoir, George wrote that the big conferences and Notre Dame, which dominated every aspect of the college game, resented Penn State for its schedule and Paterno for his outspokenness.

"Many people said 'the good old boys' didn't want this 'wop' to prove you could win a national championship with his rebellious attitudes toward the existing NCAA structure," George wrote.

Periodically, in part to help counter that perceived resentment toward Eastern football, talk about an Eastern league surfaced. Paterno would become the concept's most vocal advocate. But until one was created, there was nothing he could do to upgrade Penn State's ranking except to upgrade its schedule. That job got easier after 1973.

"They are standing in line for us," Penn State athletic director Ed Czekaj said that year about possible opponents. "For the first time, Penn State can be selective."

In the next dozen-plus years, Penn State loaded up its schedule with such nontraditional foes as Alabama, Notre Dame, Texas A&M, Nebraska, TCU, Houston, and Missouri. The strategy worked. In the 1980s, Penn State would capture a pair of national titles and, if not forever quashing the "East is Least" talk, at least separating itself for good from the rest of the region's teams.

The reasons for that altered perception, as a *Daily Collegian* sportswriter noted that same year, were Paterno, the success of his teams and his Grand Experiment, and the school's new and improved image. Or, in a single word, Paterno.

But in 1973, the coach was prepared for the familiar end-of-season frustration. After the Orange Bowl victory, he told reporters, "This was the best team I've ever coached. We have as much right to claim the top place as anyone else. We're undefeated.... I have my own poll, the Paterno poll. I took the vote a few minutes ago, and the vote was unanimous: Penn State is number one."

The coach ordered rings for his players and presented them before graduation. Each ring contained the player's name, the 12–0 record, and a replica of the Orange Bowl trophy. "It was a nice gesture," said quarterback Tom Shuman. "All of us felt like we were as good as any team in the country."

• • •

In what many then and later would label a down year for the award, Cappelletti won the Heisman Trophy that December. Regardless of the reasons, it was a breakthrough. No player from Penn State, which historically got little Heisman respect from non-Eastern voters, had ever won.

Even though Cappelletti received no help from the South— four rivals got more votes in that region—his victory indicated that the Nittany Lions were broadening their national image. That it came so soon after Paterno's much-heralded January decision and his widely quoted commencement talk was not a coincidence.

In this case, however, whatever benefits Penn State derived from Cappelletti's Heisman would be trumped by the reaction that followed the running back's memorable acceptance speech.

On the night of December 13, 1973, in the ballroom of the New York Hilton, a crowd of 700 attended the award presentation. Vice President Gerald Ford sat at the dais with Paterno. So did former Heisman winners, various coaches, and Archbishop Fulton Sheen, the theatrical silver-tongued Catholic prelate whose weekly television show had been hugely popular in the 1950s.

Cappelletti's parents from the Philadelphia suburb of Upper Darby also were there, seated at a front-row table along with his siblings, including 11-year-old Joey, who was fatally ill with leukemia.

A few months earlier, on October 27 in what in retrospect seems like a scene from a bad movie, Cappelletti had promised Joey that for his 11th birthday, John would score four touchdowns against West Virginia. He had three before Paterno, always sensitive about running up a score, sat him down in the second half of a game the Lions would win 62–14.

Cappelletti wouldn't say anything, but teammates who knew of his pledge did. They informed the coach, who sent his star back out. He scored the fourth touchdown, then retreated permanently to the bench.

Paterno would call the tough but tender-hearted Cappelletti one of the best players and people he'd ever coached. But the prospect of making a speech at the Downtown Athletic Club banquet before an audience that would be peppered with jaded New York reporters terrified the player. "This was just a big old kid from Philadelphia who wasn't a public speaker by any stretch of the imagination," lineman Mark Markovich said.

The Thursday of the banquet, with the help of his brother, Marty, a journalism major at Temple, Cappelletti put together the outline of a speech. At the bottom of the last page, he made a notation in bold letters, "JOEY."

His would be the last of the night's many speeches. Wearing a tuxedo, augmented with a big 1970s-style bow tie, a ruffled shirt, and a white nametag on his breast pocket, Cappelletti walked to the microphone at the center of the three-tiered dais.

He began routinely enough, thanking his family and his coach at Monsignor Bonner High. Then he moved on to Paterno, noting that the coach, seated behind him and to his right, had met Joey on his first recruiting visit to his home.

"When he came in the door, he looked over and on the couch was my brother, Joseph, lying there," said Cappelletti. "He was very ill at the time, more so than usual…and Coach Paterno was more concerned and talked more about what he could do for my brother than what he could do to get me at Penn State.

"I think everyone here knows about [Paterno's] coaching accomplishments at Penn State," he said. "His record is a great one, probably the greatest in the country.… [But] he's more concerned with young people after they get out of school than when they are in school—what he can do for them to make better lives for them.... I don't think there is a more dedicated man anywhere concerned with young people and a better teacher of life on and off the field."

The player than mentioned his teammates and backfield coach Phillips before turning to the paragraph that would generate a best-selling book, one that nearly 40 years later is still read by middle-school students. The story also became a Golden Globe–nominated television movie and still produces heartfelt tears in hard men.

"The youngest member of my family, Joseph, is very ill," Cappelletti said, trying to fight back tears and to keep from looking at the family table. "He has leukemia."

At that point, noted Paterno, all fidgeting in the large room ceased. No glasses rattled. There were no whispered remarks. Waiters and waitresses stopped in their tracks. "You could have heard a pin drop," Paterno said.

"If I can dedicate this trophy to him tonight and give him a couple of days of happiness, this is worth everything," Cappelletti continued. "I think a lot of people think that I go through a lot on Saturdays and during the week as most athletes do, and you get your bumps and bruises and it is a terrific battle out there on the field. Only for me, it is on Saturdays and it's only in the fall. For Joseph, it is all year round, and it is a battle that is unending with him, and he puts up with much more than I'll ever put up with, and I think that this trophy is more his than mine because he has been a great inspiration to me."

By then Cappelletti could barely control his emotions. The sobs and sniffles were audible throughout the ballroom of a hotel located in the capital of cynicism. Vice President Ford, who in a typically bumbling speech had called the award winner "Joe Cappelletti" and his coach "my good friend John Fraterno," also was in tears.

At the Cappelletti table, the player's father consoled his sobbing wife. Also seated there was another teammate, Ed O'Neil. "When it was over," O'Neil recalled, "I couldn't find the strength in my legs to stand up."

Paterno, for one of the few times in public, removed his glasses. He dabbed at his eyes repeatedly. As sad as the situation was, he was proud of Cappelletti. With the spotlight on him, he had turned it away, pointing it at a brother in need. If Paterno's Grand Experiment had a high point, that might have been it.

Archbishop Sheen was also misty-eyed when, waiting for the long ovation that followed Cappelletti's speech to end, he rose to deliver the benediction.

"Maybe for the first time in your lives," Sheen began, "you have heard a speech from the heart and not from the lips. Part of John's triumph was made by Joseph's sorrow. You don't need a blessing. God has already blessed you in John Cappelletti."

Joey Cappelletti would keep that Heisman Trophy in his bedroom for the rest of his short life. He would die on April 8, 1976, with his beloved big brother by his side.

Later on the night of the Heisman banquet, at a Penn State reception in one of the hotel's penthouse suites, Paterno bumped into Patriots owner Billy Sullivan.

"Do you see now why I couldn't leave?" Paterno asked.

"Yes," said Sullivan, "I think I do."

10

As Paterno made his way back to State College that Friday morning after the emotional Heisman dinner, he must have felt closer than ever to the national championship he'd been chasing so long.

It had to happen soon, didn't it? He and his Penn State program were winning games at an astounding pace, attracting unprecedented attention and athletes and gaining new converts daily.

Happy Valley had become a Holy Land inhabited by a saint and his pure-as-snow disciples. Who could possibly deny them a national title? What parents of a high school football player would resist pushing their son in that direction?

The heartwarming Cappelletti story—coverage of which was ubiquitous in newspapers and on television broadcasts that December weekend—would cast an even warmer glow on Penn State's football success and the Grand Experiment. As Paterno told several interviewers the previous night, he couldn't have been prouder.

But pride, as the Psalmist noted, often precedes the fall. No one could have foreseen what awaited Paterno in the remainder of the decade. Though he would exit the 1970s still standing, still swinging, and in most respects still as strong as ever, he would also be badly bruised and still without a championship.

He would have to endure a frightening personal scare involving his oldest son, a showdown with an idol that resulted in the most painful defeat of his career, and a fraying of the reputation he had so carefully constructed.

That last development, the details of which were chronicled in a 1980 *Sports Illustrated* story that used a Paterno quote for its title ("There Are a Lot of People Who Think I'm a Phony and Now They Think They Have Proof") secretly gladdened the hearts of many Penn State rivals.

"He's told too many people too long how to run their programs," said Pitt's Jackie Sherrill, himself the target of an infamous Paterno putdown, to *The New York Times* in 1979. "Now look. Penn State plays great football and always will under Joe. I just hope now they will stop criticizing all of us for being human, too."

• • •

Penn State would follow the unbeaten 1973 season with a 26–10 record over the next three years. A Cotton Bowl victory over Baylor concluded a 10–2 season in 1974 for the 10th-ranked Nittany Lions; they'd end up No. 8 in 1975 with a 9–3 record that included a Sugar Bowl loss to Alabama; another bowl loss to another traditional football power, Notre Dame in the Gator, ended a disappointing 1976 season at 7–5.

Paterno knew that with an ever-changing cast of players, it was virtually impossible to compete for a national title every year. But he also understood recruiting well enough to realize that with the right mix of experience and inexperience, you could build a contender every few years.

It looked as if 1977 might be one of those years. Penn State was 4–1 heading into an October 15 game at Syracuse. Matt Suhey, the bruising son of Paterno's early State College landlords, was bowling people over, and quarterback Chuck Fusina showed real promise. On the other side, players like Matt Millen and Bruce Clark were helping Paterno build one of his best defenses.

But on October 14, as he prepared to depart for Syracuse, the coach got a call at home from the principal of Our Lady of Victory, his children's school. His 11-year-old son, David, had tumbled off a trampoline and landed head-first on a concrete floor.

Paterno rushed to the school and found the boy unconscious. He was taken to Centre Community Hospital, and doctors there determined David had fractured his skull. Fearing permanent paralysis or worse, they urged a transfer to Geisinger Medical Center in Danville. An ambulance was summoned, and the coach made the 65-mile trip alongside his son.

"It was the longest ride of my life," Paterno said. "Every mile I concentrated on prayers, simply begging God to keep my son alive."

Though still unconscious—he would remain in a coma for seven days—David Paterno had stabilized enough that night that his father thought briefly that he might still be able to get to Syracuse.

"The last word we had was that Joe planned to fly in about noon," Bob Phillips told reporters after the game. Phillips, along with Sandusky, replaced Paterno for the game. "But David took a turn for the worse...and [Joe] called about 10:00 AM and said he wasn't coming."

The 31–24 victory over the Orangemen would be the first game Paterno had missed as head coach and just his second absence at Penn State. (The first was for his father's funeral in 1955.)

"At times like that," he said, "you start to reevaluate your life and put your priorities in order.… Nothing in this world means anything to me like my son."

The boy regained consciousness the following week, and Paterno was back at practice. Miraculously, David would recover and suffer no permanent damage.

The Paternos by then had five children—all between ages five and 15—and had recently purchased a ranch home in College Heights, the neighborhood where the coach had bunked with Engle during his first days in State College.

The four-bedroom home, more contemporary than most others on dead-end McKee Street, abutted Sunset Park. Paterno eventually would customize the interior to his needs, creating a first-floor office/den whose high windows opened to the park, and putting a bar in the basement that soon became *the* place for Happy Valley gatherings.

On Friday nights, the coach hosted a basement gathering for sportswriters and other weekend visitors. Then on Saturday nights when the Nittany Lions played at home, it was the scene for another get-together, this one featuring the Italian cooking that Sue Paterno had learned from her mother-in-law.

When asked what her husband's favorite food was, Sue said, "Anything covered with red sauce." The rigatoni, spaghetti, lasagna, sausage and meatballs attracted family, friends, ex-players, scouts, and even opposing coaches. Minnesota's coach Glen Mason recalled being invited to the Paternos after his Gophers had beaten Penn State in a game they'd begun with a successful onside kick.

"We went downstairs, and he fixed me a drink," Mason recalled. "[Then] he said to me, 'I want to tell you one thing— starting a game with an onside kick is cheating.'"

Paterno even worked on Sundays when he only occasionally made it to Mass. Raised a Catholic and a devoted Latin student, he resented it when the changes imposed by Vatican II included the vernacular Mass—with English replacing Latin in the U.S.— and decided he now could establish his own rules. The church, like college football, was not immune to his critical scrutiny.

"Somehow that freed me to make decisions on my own," he said. "Whether I liked a particular priest or whether I felt like listening to his sermon.... I have trouble accepting that what's right on one day...[is] suddenly not right or not necessary the next day."

Meal times, generally at 7:00 or 7:30, were often the only occasions when the children got to see and talk with their father. Paterno preferred working at home to his office, but while ensconced in his den he was lost in a fog of Xs and Os, game film, phone calls, and details.

The pace didn't slow much in the off-season when the coach frequently was gone on recruiting trips or, especially after 1973, speaking engagements. Paterno was in demand for everything from Pop Warner League banquets to corporate retreats. Between those and the opportunities for commercials and product endorsements that arose, he eventually hired a Cleveland firm, Keating Management Agency, to represent him.

Paterno was extremely selective about commercial opportunities, turning down many lucrative ones or with others often working out deals that financially benefitted Penn State more than himself.

Fundraising for the school's athletic and academic sides, schmoozing with donors and alumni, upgrading minor Penn State events into happenings with his star presence, Paterno was Penn State's omnipresent dynamo. "It sounds corny, I guess... but I'd like to see Penn State No. 1 in everything," he said.

Charities and nonprofits sought the aid of the man who had become the commonwealth's most recognizable citizen. He would be affiliated with such organizations as the Boy Scouts, the American Cancer Society, and the Multiple Sclerosis Foundation.

But all of that took time away from his family.

"If there was a father-daughter thing, I'd go with the neighbors," said daughter Mary Kay Hort, the second oldest child. "He didn't participate in a lot of those things."

Sometimes it wasn't by choice. When Paterno attended one of his children's—or later grandchildren's—school or sports activities, he'd often be swamped by well-wishers.

"As far back as our first undefeated season, 1968, I found out I could no longer relate normally to my own children," he said.

The coach encountered the same thing wherever he went, whether it was to Jay's football games, Diana's cheerleading, Mary Kay's gymnastics competitions, Scott's ice hockey games, or even to a restaurant, lecture, or the supermarket. So he stopped going.

At a basketball game where he was scheduled to present an award, Paterno rose from his seat and precipitated an ovation from the crowd—even though he was just walking to the men's room.

The coach recognized the price he was paying for football success. But he had no choice. He was, after all, fulfilling the destiny that had summoned him here 30 years before.

"I can remember things that happened 20 years ago in football games," he would say ruefully, "but I can't remember what my kids did."

Jay, who would be the only football-playing Paterno child and who now is a member of his father's staff, said when it wasn't the public's interest it was football that prevented his father from attending significant events in Jay's life.

"I had a [high school] football banquet," Jay said, "and Dad couldn't be there because it was the Friday before we played Pitt. Obviously I understood that, but it didn't make me happy."

Paterno readily admitted that he didn't golf or fish, and he had no hobbies. Football consumed him. Sometimes, particularly after a tough loss or a disappointing season, he needed to immerse himself in it without distractions.

Paterno purchased a home on the southern New Jersey shore in the tiny resort town of Avalon. When the weather was nice, the coach would retreat there for serious thinking, on and off the beach. His focus often would be so intense there, Hort said, that he'd use one dish and one glass, washing them over and over again.

Sue Paterno had become his buffer. She screened the calls, kept the kids quiet, did the routine chores, and made Joe's zealous devotion to football possible. So completely did Joe come to depend on her that when his wife went out of town, he was lost domestically.

With no kitchen skills, he'd sometimes try to order a pizza for dinner. The problem was, according to Jay, when he gave his name, the person on the other end invariably thought it was a prank and hung up.

But when there was free time at home, his children said, Paterno was a loving, strict, and dutiful father. He'd get into philosophical discussions with them, walk them to the bus, ask about their schoolwork, read to them, challenge their opinions, and establish rigid ground rules for their behavior.

And on rare occasions, the children got a chance to watch him prepare for a game, to witness firsthand his focus and determination.

Scott Paterno, an attorney now, recalled how his father charted a 2006 Temple–Penn State game off the television when he was at home recuperating from a broken leg.

"My father approaches coaching like a game of chess where the relative strength of the pieces changes from year to year, presenting a constantly challenging task of achieving fixed goals through forever-evolving tactics, limited by the resources at his disposal, bounded by the rules of the game, yet unfettered in its capacity to captivate a truly special intellect," Scott said.

Just as Joe Paterno tried whenever possible to avoid the trappings of wealth and fame, he shielded his children from it, as well. He didn't buy them cars. They didn't have a pool. They all had jobs. They raked the leaves. And they were off limits to reporters.

Paterno, on the other hand, was always available. The coach's telephone number was listed in the borough's phone book, and everyone in town knew where he lived. There was no fence around Paterno's property, which abutted a public park.

Even when his salary increased to more than $1 million a year in the 2000s, Paterno would remain in the McKee Street house, insisting it was more than he needed. The money he might have spent on a new one, he liked to say, would work more good as a donation to Penn State or some charity.

All five children would graduate from Penn State, where Paterno's position as a tenured professor earned him a 75 percent reduction in their tuition.

• • •

A surprising home loss to Kentucky 24–20 was the only blemish on the 1977 team's 11–1 record. Paterno and his returning players were convinced that Penn State could compete for a national title the following season.

After starting out with an unexpectedly close win over Temple in Philadelphia, his Lions began to beat up on opponents. They shut out fifth-ranked Ohio State in Columbus 19–0 and held TCU (58–0) and Kentucky (30–0) scoreless in routs.

Following a win over unbeaten Maryland, quarterback Chuck Fusina even made the cover of *Sports Illustrated*. A week later, after defeating North Carolina State 19–10, the Nittany Lions became the nation's No. 1 team for the first time in school history. Fusina believed the polls and publicity were related.

"Sometimes that's what it takes," Fusina said. "Some people see [the cover of the national magazine] and they recognize that team may not be too bad out there. They were paying attention to us after that."

They validated that lofty standing in their season finale, defeating Pitt to improve to 11–0. With his team top-ranked now, Paterno wanted to avoid another 1969-like debacle. He carefully weighed his bowl options. More than anything he wanted to ensure that if the Lions won, they'd be champions and that the title wouldn't go to some other bowl's winner as had happened with Texas.

Realizing the value of an Orange Bowl telecast—as the only night game on New Year's Day, it invariably drew enormous audiences—Paterno had hoped for a matchup there with

Billy Sims and run-happy Oklahoma. The Nittany Lions were particularly good at stopping the run. But the appeal of that pairing had been diminished somewhat when Nebraska beat the unbeaten Sooners in their annual Thanksgiving week shootout.

Though he wouldn't admit it, Paterno was understandably wary about having to beat the shrewd Bear Bryant and his Alabama team, which was ranked No. 2. The two schools had matched up in the Sugar Bowl three years earlier, and Alabama had won 13–6. But Bryant turned on the charm and after several calls to the Penn State coach convinced him to bring his boys to New Orleans again.

The matchup between No. 1 and No. 2 was set, a pairing the media painted as a meeting of the new master and the old, North vs. South, horned-rims vs. houndsteeth. More significantly, after years of complaining about the polls and their anti-Eastern bias, the pressure was on Paterno. He finally had his chance to win a national title on the field.

In New Orleans that last week of December, Paterno couldn't shake the strange spell Bryant cast on him. If he wasn't intimidated, he was at least constantly aware of his aura. "Even his peers in the coaching business felt in awe of him," Paterno said of Bryant. "He had such charisma. Whatever it is that makes great generals, he had it. Tons of it. He was just a giant figure."

Their first encounter had come a quarter-century earlier in an elevator at a coaches convention. Bound for his fourth-floor room one night, Paterno boarded. There the unknown assistant found himself surrounded by some of the sport's biggest coaching names—Oklahoma's Bud Wilkinson, Notre Dame's recently retired Frank Leahy, Georgia's Wally Butts, and Bryant, who was at that time at Texas A&M.

Awestruck, Paterno rode past his floor just so he could bask in their presence. A day later, he attended a lecture by Bryant, "one of the best clinic speeches I had ever heard."

"He didn't have a lot to say," Paterno recalled, "but he said a couple of things…about game plans. 'Keep your plan small. Have a plan for everything.'" That last tip impressed the younger coach, who forever after would make detailed notes for himself and others.

A few years later at the inaugural Liberty Bowl in 1959, Penn State beat Alabama 7–0. Paterno was still an assistant, but after he succeeded Engle, he would face off with Bryant's Alabama four times between 1975 and 1982—and lose them all.

For this national title game in the new Louisiana Superdome, on its rock-hard artificial turf, Paterno's team and Bryant's team tore into each other with a frenzy that matched the noise from the sold-out crowd. Alabama led 14–7 when with just more than 7 minutes to play in the fourth quarter, Matt Millen forced a fumble and Penn State recovered at the Crimson Tide's 19-yard line.

On second-and-goal from the 6-yard line, Fusina hit Scott Fitzkee at the three. Penn State's receiver seemed to be clear but just shy of the goal line, then Alabama cornerback Don McNeal flashed into the picture and stopped Fitzkee 2 feet short. "I have no idea where that Alabama back came from," Fitzkee said afterward.

Suhey got the ball next. As the big fullback slammed into the line, the entire Alabama defense met him. Paterno would always believe the fullback reached the end zone but, with less than 2 minutes left, the officials signaled fourth down.

Paterno called for a timeout. He didn't want any mistakes. This, he would say, was "my destined chance to outcoach a legend." Assuming Bryant, a man Paterno had called a defensive genius, would be ready for a another plunge or a quarterback sneak, he wanted Fusina to fake a handoff and toss the ball to tight end Mickey Shuler.

"A couple of my soundest coaches insisted I play the percentages—just crash through the couple of feet for a touchdown," Paterno wrote. "With an eerie clarity, I still remember the sure voice of my instinct: 'That's a lot of crap. This is the time to surprise them and throw the football.'

"But I didn't say it out loud. Instead, I paused for a most finely split moment to hear another voice in my head. 'Hold it, Joe. What if…' That moment was one of the few in my life when I backed off from a strong instinct and let myself worry about what people might say if the decision was wrong."

He acceded to his assistants' wishes and told Fusina to give the ball to Mike Guman. The tailback would run behind All-American tackle Keith Dorney and, if there was no hole, vault himself into the end zone.

After Suhey's failed effort, Fusina had asked the referee how far the ball was from the end zone. The official told him it was about a foot. "Then you'd better pass for it!" Alabama defensive end Marty Lyons yelled at the quarterback.

Guman got the handoff and jumped toward a goal line that already had vanished beneath a mountain of red and white. Lineman Murray Legg hit Guman low, while linebacker Barry Krause hit Guman high. Krause, in fact, struck Guman so hard that he cracked his red helmet along its seam.

Guman didn't make it, and Alabama got the ball. But still it wasn't over. Penn State held, forcing the Tide to punt. After a bad snap, Woody Umphrey shanked the kick and the ball dribbled out of bounds near Alabama's 30.

Then in what must have been some eerie cosmic payback for their good fortune in the 1969 Orange Bowl, a flag fluttered onto the turf. Penn State was penalized for having too many men on the field. Reprieved, Alabama was able to virtually run out the clock, winning the game and the national title Paterno so coveted.

When it was over, the heartbreak among Penn State's players, coaches, and fans was palpable. Millen left the building almost immediately without even showering. "I just changed and walked back to the hotel," he said. "I was disgusted."

So was his coach.

"I have talked about getting angry with myself when I lose," Paterno wrote in his autobiography. "Nothing of the kind ever compared to that loss.... It got me. It hammered at my ego. When I stood toe to toe with Bear Bryant, he outcoached me."

Once again, George Paterno sensed something sinister in the painful defeat. His brother had long sermonized about the evils in college sports. Many believed the teams in Alabama's conference, the SEC (often derided as standing for "Surely Everybody Cheats"), were the worst offenders, and thus most resentful of Paterno's preaching.

"It was rumored every coach in the conference was offering information to Bear Bryant about how to beat Penn State," George Paterno wrote. "It was the South, coached by the kingfish of the 'good old boys,' against the extremely confident, annoying, skinny 'wop' leader from the East."

• • •

Someone must have punctured Penn State's balloon at the moment Guman was stopped amid that sea of white-hot noise inside the Superdome.

The air leaked out steadily and sometimes dramatically from the high-flying program in 1979, a year in which Paterno and his philosophy would be challenged and criticized as never before.

His Nittany Lions would lose four times at Beaver Stadium, finishing what had seemed a promising season with a disappointing 8–4 mark. His players would be in and out of trouble all year (mostly in). Beaver Stadium fans even booed Paterno, particularly his conservative play-calling. Paterno's brother, a color analyst on Penn State radio broadcasts, acknowledged that Joe needed "to open up the offense."

"Well," Penn State professor Milton Bergstein said that year, "I guess we were due for a little bad luck."

The strange thing was that no one had seen it coming. When the tough-minded news show *60 Minutes* profiled Paterno and his team late in the 1978 season, the portrayal was positively Pollyanna-ish. "We only do shows like that on guys who die," one surprised CBS staffer complained to *Sports Illustrated*.

Trouble blew in to State College and lingered like a stubborn Nor'easter. Lineman Todd Hodne was arrested in connection with a rape in the summer of 1979, and he would be booted off the team. Nine years later he would be convicted in the murder of a New York cab driver.

Fall practice began with an announcement from Paterno that three defensive players were academically ineligible, including All-American safety Pete Harris, the younger brother of NFL star Franco. "He was a goof-off in high school, and he was a goof-off here," Paterno explained. "What could I do about it? I don't care whose brother he was."

Meanwhile, during a grueling practice run, Matt Millen failed to finish. When his coach ordered him to continue, he said he couldn't. Paterno stripped Millen of his captaincy, but the incident and those that followed continued to destabilize the team.

University police cited two offensive linemen, starter Bill Dugan and reserve Bob Hladun, for drinking beer while they sat on a campus bench. "The stupidity of it drives me up a wall," Paterno said. Both were suspended for the Texas A&M game, which the Nittany Lions lost.

Tailback Leo McClelland, frustrated by a lack of playing time, quit not long afterward, and at midseason tailback Booker Moore, who had run for a career-best 166 yards that same afternoon, was arrested for drunk driving after cracking up his car. He was suspended for the Miami game, which was another loss.

Fullback Dave Paffenroth got involved in a campus fight and was suspended for a game. Finally, while the team was in Memphis for the Liberty Bowl, tight end Bill LeBlanc left the hotel, wandered into a private house while allegedly looking for a place to sleep, and had a bullet fired at him by the frightened owner. He was charged with burglary.

What was going on here? Was this an aberrant year? Or had the lid finally been lifted on Happy Valley? No one was quite certain.

"Suddenly it seemed like we were all a bunch of felons down here," said Dave Baker, the Penn State sports information director at the time.

Paterno denied that these kinds of things had always happened. "We have never covered up things around here," he said. "We just didn't have problems." Players like Pittman backed him up.

But to paraphrase Bob Dylan, who was experiencing his own existential angst at the time, something was happening here and no one knew what it was...did they, Mister Jones?

Even Paterno was forced to admit that the "Grand Experiment is kind of in disrepute."

• • •

As the incidents piled up, you could almost hear the gleeful chuckling from Paterno's coaching colleagues. St. Joe, the outspoken critic, the pompous pontificator, was getting his at last.

That view of Paterno was exacerbated early in the 1979 season when, during one of his Friday night sessions with the media, he was asked if he planned to capitalize on his fame by getting into politics.

"I'm not going to give up college football to the Jackie Sherrills and Barry Switzers of the world," Paterno said, referencing the problems, real and rumored, that had attached themselves to the Pitt and Oklahoma coaches, respectively.

The comment was made in an off-the-record setting, but on this occasion someone—no one has ever been certain which of the 15 or so writers present—leaked it. Bob Smizik, a Pittsburgh sportswriter who covered Sherrill's team, heard about it, asked the offended coach for a response, and printed the story. Paterno was furious and briefly ended the weekly gab sessions.

What was going on? "This was no University of New Mexico. This was Penn State, holier-than-thou Pennsylvania State University, where Billy Budd would have to prove himself before being issued shoulder pads," *Sports Illustrated*'s Looney wrote.

Brother George was asked if, as Paterno's critics claimed, the coach was too pious. "Absolutely," he said. "If you don't wear a backward collar, it's hard to get away with piety."

Even Paterno himself was forced to acknowledge that perhaps he'd laid it on a bit thick while things were going well, though in doing so he apparently couldn't resist citing another college football problem.

"I don't like to put myself up as a do-gooder, but I am," Paterno said. "We have an obligation to try to make these athletes better people. If a kid goes through here and can't read and write but can knock people down, is that good? We've got more of an obligation than that."

Some suggested Paterno was a hypocrite. After all, for years he had spoken of the need to keep freshmen ineligible, noting that incoming collegians needed to make an academic and social adjustment before having to worry about varsity football. But when the rule was changed in 1972 and freshmen became eligible, Paterno, like all of his silent colleagues, played them— though he would always admit to a certain reluctance.

"I hate the freshman-eligible rule.... If I had enough guts, I'd say that regardless [of the rule], freshmen aren't going to play here. But that's how I'm hypocritical. I don't say that because it would hurt our recruiting and our football team.... There is hypocrisy in me and a little of the con man and actor, too. Look, I'm not trying to fool anybody."

His players stood by him, even if most did admit that with his constant carping at practices and his whiny admonishments about even the smallest misstep, he could be difficult.

"I enjoyed playing for him much more after I was through playing for him," Lydell Mitchell told *Sports Illustrated*. Charlie Pittman said, "There is not any like or love for Joe.... What Joe wants is your best effort, that's all." And Bruce Clark added, "If a guy wants friends, he can go bowling; if he wants to win in big-time competition, sacrifices must be made."

Those three players were black. So were the three defenders who became academically ineligible in 1979, a development that reopened the debate about how inviting lily-white Happy Valley was for minorities.

Sports Illustrated reported that five black Penn State players had been admitted through the special program Paterno and Oswald had established to help more blacks qualify. All met NCAA standards (a 2.0 high school average) but not Penn State's guidelines. Only one performed poorly enough to warrant a suspension, Paterno said, while the other four did well.

"We are fighting a lily-white look here," Paterno explained. "And among that group of five that I asked to have specially admitted, only one was a super high school athlete. As for the other four, we easily could have gotten white players as good or better who were fully qualified."

The entrance standards for football players of any color were more relaxed than those for non-athletes at Penn State. And once accepted, all could avail themselves of any tutoring help they needed.

"I don't think it's anything to be ashamed of that we want to help," Paterno said.

There could be no arguing with Penn State's success in graduating its athletes. According to the NFL Player Register for 1979, of the 31 Penn State players in the league that year, 29 had undergraduate degrees. In the entire NFL, only 611 of the 1,690 players had graduated.

11

WHATEVER PENN STATE'S FOOTBALL PROBLEMS may have been in 1980, they weren't going to be resolved by increasing Paterno's workload. Always obsessively compulsive about his duties, the longer he coached, the less free time he had and the more demands there were.

"One of the problems that you get the longer you're in it [is that there are] more friends and kids and people who count on you," Paterno said. "Your time away from coaching gets more and more significant. People have funerals, [ex-]players have kids who need a hand, the whole band of people you're involved with stretches a little bit more. That's when you start to get swamped. You keep thinking it won't hurt here, it won't hurt there. [Then] you wake up one morning and you have a crappy organization."

Squeezing even a few more minutes from his busy days seemed inconceivable. And yet, on January 14, 1980, with the kind of secrecy that was becoming a trademark there, an official Penn State press release announced that in addition to coaching the football team Paterno would be the university's new athletic director. It was stunning news.

The combination coach/AD wasn't rare at big-time football schools, particularly in the South. Alabama's Bear Bryant and

Texas' Darrell Royal, for example, held both positions. But in their cases, it was generally conceded that the extra title was more ceremonial, more an acknowledgement that football ruled at those schools, more a means to consolidate power, more a way to fatten their wallets and egos.

Paterno, meanwhile, had always decried such arrangements as excessive, insisting money and power didn't interest him. Now he, too, appeared to be creating or at least consolidating his own football empire. *Et tu*, Joe?

Nothing about the move made sense. Throughout 1979, Paterno had accepted blame for his team's off-the-field difficulties. His job, he explained, had become so all-consuming that he'd lost the ability to form close relationships with his players.

Now in addition to a 24/7 coaching job, Paterno was going to be the athletic director at a large state university. If he took the new job seriously—and no one suspected that the earnest Paterno would do anything else—he would be overseeing a multimillion-dollar budget, 30-plus men's and women's sports, scores of department employees, dozens of coaches, hundreds of players, plus all the related academic, financial, eligibility, scheduling, and personnel responsibilities that went along with the position.

The athletic director role might have made sense if Paterno had been planning to step away from football, but he clearly had no plans to do that despite claiming in 1978, for the first of many times, that he'd "probably coach another four or five years and then get out."

Paterno was replacing Ed Czekaj, who had become his alma mater's athletic director when Ernie McCoy retired in 1969. A member of the Cotton Bowl team in 1947, Czekaj was now 60 and being shoved aside, although he was given the title of special assistant to Robert Patterson, the senior vice president for finance and operations. Robert Scannell, dean of the College of Health and Physical Education, appeared to be an even bigger loser in the shakeup. The former athletic department head now was subservient to both Czekaj and Paterno. The vague press release revealed that Paterno would report to Patterson on budgetary matters and to Scannell on admissions and eligibility issues.

Questions, both immediate and long-term, were raised: How could Paterno manage two immensely complex jobs? Was this a coach-engineered coup? Was there now anyone in the reshuffled department strong enough to oppose Paterno when he wanted improved facilities or a bigger football budget? And why now? What role did 1979's problems play? Was it merely a ceremonial title meant to reward the coach? Exactly what duties would he perform? And if he didn't perform them, who would?

Answers would not be easily forthcoming, then or later. Incredibly for a personnel shift of this magnitude, involving as it did the university's best-known figure, Penn State conducted no news conference. Phone messages from reporters to administrators were not returned. Paterno barely addressed the subject in his 1989 autobiography. Decades later, the reasons remain mysterious.

"We were in a little bit of a transitional situation," Paterno would say years later in a cryptic evaluation of the move. "The reason I took over was...we had been to four or five straight New Year's Day bowls as an independent, and I was trying to get some facilities done and we didn't have any money. It was a lot of late nights until 3:00 or 4:00 AM.... There still were some things that were not right. It wasn't anybody's fault, but that is just the way it drifted a little bit. So I took it over."

President John Oswald would later try to explain the move by saying money had become increasingly important in college sports and that finances and budgets were not Czekaj's strengths. But were they Paterno's strengths? And how willing would the head football coach/AD be to share the $5.5 million his team would generate in 1980 with, say, women's field hockey, especially since he then doubted the whole concept of female athletes?

In the absence of any hard and official information, speculation was rampant. Paterno was given an expanded role to keep him from taking one of the NFL jobs he periodically was offered. Paterno, fearful that Title IX reforms might threaten his program, was grabbing the power, ensuring that his would be the final say on any decision involving football. Paterno had won a power struggle with Czekaj and Scannell. Paterno wanted more money. Paterno had lost his mind.

Both Paterno and Oswald later denied all those theories without providing an alternate rationale. In a 2004 interview, Patterson suggested the coach neither sought nor wanted the AD's job. But with Czekaj being pushed aside, Patterson said, there was no heir-apparent. The coach merely stepped in until a replacement could be found.

That's difficult to accept when you consider that the man who ultimately got the job, Jim Tarman, had been there all along, and that he was as close to Paterno as anyone at the university.

In any event, it would be Tarman who, in his new role as associate AD, would perform most of the job's day-to-day functions. Paterno would be consulted on the significant issues, especially those that impacted his team.

Paterno's brief reign as AD was not entirely uneventful. Beaver Stadium's seating capacity, not surprisingly, would swell to 87,770 as football's essential role as department breadwinner grew ever more clear.

Paterno, who banned female reporters—and as a consequence all reporters—from his locker room, would be among the first at Penn State to tackle the dilemmas created by Title IX, the 1972 federal legislation that mandated equal opportunities for female athletes.

Raised before World War II, Paterno initially shared his generation's patronizing views toward women. He could be condescending when discussing female athletes and the sports they played, so much so that he later felt it necessary to apologize for having once stated that women didn't really know "what competition meant."

Several court rulings involving Title IX soon made it clear that schools were going to have to provide an equal number of scholarships for men and women. That put all men's sports in jeopardy. Paterno fought hard—but failed—to remove football from any solution. "I'm for everything Title IX wants to do except giving them an equal number or percentage of scholarships," he said in 1975.

Ultimately, the issue that consumed most of Paterno's energies as athletic director was the creation of an Eastern sports conference, one that would rival those poll-powerful leagues in other regions. Paterno's failure to successfully do so would be one of his career's signature failures.

In 1976, the Eastern Eight conference began play in basketball. Penn State was one of its original members, along with Villanova, Duquesne, West Virginia, George Washington, Massachusetts, Pitt, and Rutgers. But the young league had two fatal flaws—too many schools where football didn't exist or was threatened, and a minor-league television contract.

Paterno knew the Eastern Eight wouldn't work for the football super-conference he envisioned. He wanted to corral Syracuse, Boston College, and Temple to join with Pitt, West Virginia, Rutgers, and Penn State in a single entity.

Meanwhile, television money was becoming the single most significant factor in college sports. The NCAA had long made the agreements and parceled out the cash. But conferences and the big independents wanted their own deals, and in 1984 the Supreme Court would give them that right. In anticipation of that change, conferences had been getting bigger and broader demographically, knowing that the larger their audiences, the larger the rights fees they could command.

The East, with several huge television markets—New York, Philadelphia, Boston, and Baltimore/Washington—in a relatively compact geographical area, was perfectly suited for such a league, even if the Eastern Eight didn't recognize it. But Providence's former basketball coach Dave Gavitt did.

In 1979, Gavitt founded the Big East, a basketball-only conference that included Providence, St. John's, Connecticut, Georgetown, Syracuse, Seton Hall, Boston College, Holy Cross, and Rutgers (which abandoned the Eastern Eight). ESPN, a new cable channel located in Connecticut, needed programming and Gavitt was happy to provide it. The two new entities eventually would grow rich together.

A year later Villanova also joined the Big East. But as successful as his new league was, Gavitt recognized that Paterno and Penn State football remained a significant wild card. To try to counter any possible move by the Nittany Lions toward the football conference Paterno wanted, Gavitt tried to lure Pitt.

If the Panthers, the East's No. 2 football power, went along with Paterno, then Boston College, Syracuse, West Virginia, and others likely would follow. The Big East could be overwhelmed.

But there had been a longstanding antagonism between Pitt and Penn State in several matters. Paterno had sniffed at Pitt's coach Jackie Sherrill's style and tactics, and the two schools bumped heads frequently while recruiting. So it wasn't a complete shock when, in 1982, Pitt announced it would be joining the Big East for basketball.

The Eastern Eight, which would later be renamed the Atlantic 8 and then the Atlantic 10, was left with the region's scraps—smaller basketball-only schools. Stymied, Paterno would never forgive Pitt. As soon as the Nittany Lions joined the Big Ten, Paterno would jettison the Panthers—a fierce and natural rival for more than a century—from his schedules.

Though the coach has long denied it, later reports indicated that in 1985 Penn State, still holding out hope for a football super-conference, applied for Big East basketball membership. The school's lackluster past in that sport and, more significantly, its out-of-the way locale—teams would have had to fly into Harrisburg in midwinter and bus 100 miles of treacherous mountain roads to State College—worked against it. By a single vote, the Big East rejected Penn State.

By then, Paterno had abandoned his second job, officially resigning as athletic director on January 18, 1982—not that he wouldn't retain control of the department. Tarman was his closest ally. And when Tarman left in 1993, Tim Curley, a former football player and another Paterno acolyte, would assume the role.

While he was no longer the athletic director, Paterno would at last become a king before a year had passed.

• • •

This must have been some sort of cruel irony, Paterno thought.

He had been here before. New Year's Day. The Sugar Bowl. The Louisiana Superdome. A Deep South opponent wearing red. No. 1 vs. No. 2. Fourth quarter. Game on the line. Penn State facing a crucial short-yardage play. Timeout.

Four years earlier at this exact spot, Paterno had been faced with virtually the same scenario. Then, on a fourth-and-1, just 1 foot away from the goal line and possible victory over Alabama in a Sugar Bowl that determined the national champ, Paterno had wanted to pass. Instead, he vetoed his gut feeling and went along with his assistants, calling for a run. Bear Bryant's defense stopped it and won a national title. The Penn State coach would kick himself forever.

By January 1, 1983, Paterno had finally heeded the cries of critics and loosened his offense. Quarterback Todd Blackledge threw for 2,218 yards in 1982 as the Nittany Lions, for one of the few times since the coach arrived in State College, gained more yards in the air than on the ground. For once, the Lions had talented wideouts, Kenny Jackson and walk-on Gregg Garrity. And gifted tailback Curt Warner would end up in the College Football Hall of Fame.

Penn State had won 10 of 11 regular-season games in 1982, including a 19–10 win over Dan Marino's fifth-ranked Pitt and a 24–14 victory at No. 13 Notre Dame. That November 13 trip to South Bend would provide another watershed moment for Paterno and his program.

When the Nittany Lions flight arrived at Notre Dame for their first ever visit, local reporters awaited. They asked, in what the coach and some players believed was a condescending manner, how it felt to be visiting this hallowed ground of college football. Penn State, the questions implied, was lucky to be there.

"We'd played a lot of big games in a lot of big places by then," said Paterno, who like most Catholic youngsters in his day, had grown up rooting for the Fighting Irish, "and I'm thinking, 'Who do these people think they are?'"

The season's lone loss did further damage to Paterno's psyche—a 42–21 defeat at Alabama. It would be Paterno's last chance at bagging the Bear. Bryant would retire after that season. Penn State's coach, to his eternal dismay, would never beat the one opponent who mattered most. The saving grace of that defeat, however, was that it came early in the season—October 9. By season's end, the 10–1 Nittany Lions had climbed up to No. 2 in the polls, just behind SEC champion Georgia.

That high ranking validated Paterno's belief that the only way the Nittany Lions were going to get more national respect was by upgrading their opponents. In 1981, when their schedule was rated the nation's toughest, the 10–2 Lions had played Nebraska, Alabama, Notre Dame, Miami, and Pitt. In 1982 they'd face all those teams again, with the exception of Miami.

Penn State and Georgia agreed to meet in a Sugar Bowl that nearly everyone conceded would produce the national champion. Even though No. 4 SMU was unbeaten, the Mustangs were relative newcomers to the poll and without the national clout necessary to leapfrog a Georgia or Penn State. "I knew how they felt," Paterno said. "I'd been there."

He was 56 now and desperate to grab this opportunity. Paterno worked his team harder than usual between their November 26 finale against Pitt and the January 1 game. Freshman running backs Eufard Cooper and Steve Smith played the role of Herschel Walker, Georgia's dynamic Heisman Trophy–winning tailback. A year earlier in a Fiesta Bowl triumph over Southern Cal, the Lions defense had shut down Marcus Allen. Paterno intended to do the same with Walker.

Time and again Cooper and Smith plunged into the teeth of a Penn State defense that Paterno was monitoring intensely and tongue-lashing frequently. Smith was so battered that he soon begged for a stand-in of his own.

Upon arriving in New Orleans, the Nittany Lions found a city awash in Georgia Bulldog fans. Garrity remarked that everywhere he went there was someone yelling, 'How 'bout them Dawgs!"

"You'd be walking down the street," Garrity recalled, "and we're poor college kids so we had to wear all of our bowl presents—the sweats and stuff—and they'd come and bark in your face."

Garrity would make the game's biggest play, stretching out to haul in a 47-yard touchdown pass from Blackledge that gave Penn State a 27–17 lead and gave *Sports Illustrated* the photo that would appear on its next cover.

But the game wasn't over. The Bulldogs turned a fumbled punt into a touchdown and they had the momentum. Now hanging onto a 27–23 lead with 1:37 to play and the ball in its own territory, Penn State faced a third-and-3.

Paterno knew he couldn't allow the Bulldogs and the explosive Walker to get the ball back. As he had done four years earlier before that pivotal fourth-and-1, he signaled for a timeout. "We had to keep the ball," he said. "We simply had to get the first down. But how?"

Since Penn State couldn't risk an interception, his assistants again urged him to call a run. Blackledge, a confident senior, said he thought he could get the yardage with a pass. Intellectually,

Paterno agreed with his aides. This time, though, he was determined to follow his gut.

"Throw it," he told Blackledge.

Blackledge hit Garrity for a 6-yard gain. Penn State kept the ball. The scoreboard turned to zeroes. Players and assistants ran for Paterno and his world became a blur—in part because his glasses had been briefly knocked off.

Suddenly, after finding Georgia's Vince Dooley for a handshake, Paterno was being carried across the field on the shoulders of his jubilant players. His tie was uncharacteristically loosened. His eyes were hidden behind the lenses of his light-sensitive glasses, darkened by the glare of the stadium's lights and camera flashes. In this moment, he permitted himself a victory smile. And though he famously forbade his players from any demonstrative gestures, Paterno pumped his right fist continually in the air.

The timing of Paterno's first title was noteworthy. He had waited 16 years as Engle's assistant before becoming head coach. Exactly 16 years later, he had won a national championship.

Was this the fulfillment of his Aeneas-like destiny? Could he now, or at some point in the not-too-distant future, walk away from coaching a contented man? What would the next 16 years bring?

That last question was interesting to contemplate. What would Joe Paterno be doing in 1998? While no one could say for sure, there probably weren't many who could have imagined that he'd still be coaching the Nittany Lions.

"Joe himself had by then begun saying that he was only going to coach another few years," Bob Mitinger recalled. "He said that after that he was going to sit in Beaver Stadium and boo the coach, whoever he was."

At the postgame party in the New Orleans Hilton, the university's long-pent-up football frustrations bubbled over into a raucous celebration. Perhaps only Paterno was subdued.

"I was getting nostalgic," he said. "I just wanted to get off in a corner for a while and remember all the players, the coaches before, who weren't around for this moment." Joe Bedenk had died in 1968, and Bob Higgins had died in 1969. Rip Engle, who was ailing, would be dead in two months.

Finally, Paterno made his way through the glad-handing throngs and went back to his room. "I didn't sleep," he said. "I just wanted to be alone."

A day later, the team's return flight was met in Harrisburg by Pennsylvania governor Dick Thornburgh. On their way back to State College, the buses passed thousands of fans from the surrounding small towns who had lined Route 322 to hail their champions. Police cars, fire engines, and private vehicles formed a celebratory escort. Horns honked, sirens blared, and voices yelled all the way to campus where 5,000 students awaited.

"I never saw such love between people who didn't know each other," Paterno said of the bus ride. "And never in one place at one time have I sensed so many football players in their private darkness sneaking so many silent, exultant tears."

The following day, Penn State's private jet flew Paterno, Blackledge, and Warner to New York for an appearance on *Good Morning America*. The players almost didn't recognize their coach. The tension of the past few weeks, the past 30-some years, had dissipated. He was relaxed and personable with them.

"It was a whole different feel to Joe that day," Blackledge recalled. "It wasn't so much like the coach-to-player thing. It was much more personal, friendly, and relaxed. I think Curt and I both got to see a side of him we had never seen before."

So did America. Paterno talked as much about Penn State the university as Penn State the national football champions. Later that same day before 15,000 fans gathered on the lawn in front of Old Main, not far from where the first football games at Penn State had been played, Paterno spoke again about how the university should seize this opportunity. Thirty-two years after coming to State College, he knew how rare such a moment was.

The ultimate Penn State triumph, he would say often in the days after the Sugar Bowl's redemption, could be greater still.

• • •

Mimi Barash Coppersmith would later characterize the speech Paterno made before her fellow university trustees on January 27, 1983, as "Penn State's Gettysburg Address."

Between the parades, banquets, speeches, ceremonies, and awards, Paterno barely took a breather after the Sugar Bowl. The trustees had invited him to their late-January meeting so that they, like virtually every other organization in Central Pennsylvania, could honor the coach.

The fact that after all those years at Penn State this would be his first appearance before the university's governing board might have added to the directness of the remarks—the stern lecture, really—he would deliver there.

After accepting a proclamation, Paterno began by noting that this was "a magic time" for Penn State. Its football team had a won a national title without cheating—"at least not deliberately." Its reputation had been burnished in the past, but now it was time to move the university up in the polls.

"It bothers me to see Penn State football number one and then to pick up a newspaper and find a report that many of our academic departments and disciplines are not rated up there with the leading institutions of the country."

The school needed to raise more money, hire better professors, improve existing departments, and create new and better ones. Penn State might no longer be the "cow college" he discovered in 1950, and its state-related status meant it was never going to be as selective as an Ivy League institution, but there was no reason it couldn't match schools like the University of Michigan, Ohio State, and Wisconsin in academic credentials.

It was all so odd. A football coach was lecturing the trustees. *Sports Illustrated*'s Rick Reilly would later joke that the speech undoubtedly marked the first time in history that "a coach yearned for a school its football team could be proud of."

While Paterno has long been a prominent Republican, he is, as his brother George noted, "socially liberal." His views of the trustees and the vision he had for Penn State could hardly have been less conservative. He called the trustees "reactionary" and implored them to create an atmosphere that encouraged "more controversy…more freedom…more people with different ideas."

With the same fervor that had marked his criticisms of college football's scoundrels, Joe Paterno went after some on the faculty ("lazy profs who are concerned only with tenure"), the lack of a clear vision from the administration, and the school's inability to compete for the best students.

A 1978 *Chronicle of Higher Education* report had revealed that the school's endowment of $11.3 million ranked 103rd among U.S. universities. A new football season, when a new No. 1 team would be crowned, was due to start in eight months, Paterno reminded them. Penn State needed to grab the moment…and grab the cash.

"We have to raise $7 to $10 million in the next six months to get up the impetus we need, or we are going to lose the opportunity," he said.

Inspired, the trustees would soon announce a $200 million campaign with Paterno as its vice chairman. The coach proved a willing and enthusiastic fund-raiser. In the decades to come, he personally would raise hundreds of millions more for Penn State.

A later Penn State president, Graham Spanier, would recall a visit he and the coach made to a major donor. The plan was for Spanier to explain the need and for Paterno to close the deal, asking for $3 million as if he were asking for a high school quarterback's signature. The coach requested $5 million instead, and the contributor immediately wrote a check for that amount.

"He understands the power of his presence," Spanier said, "and he's willing to use it for the good of the university."

Joe and Sue Paterno eventually would donate $4 million of their own to fund improvements and a new addition to the library, which now bears their name.

"I'm a little bit like Andrew Carnegie," Paterno said. "If you die with money, your life was a failure.… I really honestly believe that we have an obligation to help people who haven't been as fortunate as we have been."

Not coincidentally, football would benefit greatly from Paterno's ability to attract donors. With the Nittany Lion Club as the athletic department's fundraising arm, the team's facilities would be upgraded constantly, as would the coach's budgets for recruiting, equipment, and tutoring. The Penn State program that would grow out of 1982's success would have been unrecognizable to Engle, who passed away on March 7, 1983.

"When I first took over…we were raising $20,000 to $25,000 a year," Paterno said. "We had a guy named Cecil Spadafora from Indiana, Pennsylvania, who would give us a car, and we would raffle it off and that would get us $10,000, $12,000, $15,000.

We needed better facilities, so I'd go around trying to raise some money. I would go to different groups and say, 'I want your money, but I don't want your two cents.'"

Paterno would attract new donors as successfully as recruits. He would become not only the face of Penn State but its principal financial asset.

"I couldn't even imagine putting a dollar value on Joe Paterno," Rick Kaluza, Penn State's associate athletic director for finance, would say decades afterward.

12

As much as Paterno wanted and savored that first national title, it didn't change him as a football coach. Nothing could. No man could have a career that stretched from Patti Page to Lady Gaga without a consistent message, a consistent philosophy, and a consistent routine.

Everyone who has played for him has his own favorite JoePa story. However, whether they knew him as a young Rip Engle assistant, a new head coach, the leader of national championship teams, or an aging legend, they all experienced the same essential Joe. No matter the era, Paterno's lessons, practice rituals, annoying traits, caring nature, work habits, and quirks remained virtually unchanged.

"He never changed," said Steve Wisniewski, a mid-1980s offensive lineman. "The head coach who went 23–1 [his first two years] was no different from the head coach who went 13–10 my final two seasons. He stayed steady. He encouraged us. We prepared hard every week."

For those who have never spent much time around Paterno, the thing that often surprises them the most about the coach is how hard and harsh he can be at practices. That side of his personality is not part of the coach's public persona. St. Joe is smart, funny, righteous, and fair. The other Paterno, the one only players and aides get to see at the closed sessions, can be an unpleasant martinet.

"For the most part they think of his gentlemanly approach and the Grand Experiment," former player Matt Millen said. "But buried beneath all that stuff is a feisty little Italian…and he's not afraid to fight."

Paterno demands more during workouts than in games. He never lets up. He gets in players' faces and on their butts. Like a Marine drill sergeant, he breaks them down to build them up. He can identify a weakness—mental or physical—and zero in on it. Most players chafe until they come to sense the motive behind the madness.

"What was impressive about Joe is he knew how to motivate each individual," former lineman Mike Reid said. "And he didn't do it in a coddling way. One thing Joe never did was berate or belittle me. That would never have worked with me and for me. Joe was really brilliant at knowing what tack to take."

Paterno yells, whines, cajoles, criticizes, and threatens. He knows what everyone is supposed to be doing, and they'd better be doing it. He never lets down. He doesn't miss a thing.

He asks as much of himself, too. Paterno rises at 5:30 AM and goes until he falls asleep in bed, frequently with a pencil and notepad in his hands, jotting down some inspiration or instruction to his assistants. In between, there is little time for anything but football. Meticulously prepared, Paterno makes sure his staff knows what is expected every week, every day, and every minute.

Practice time is precious and inviolable; woe to anyone who causes an unnecessary distraction. In 2004, a Washington newspaperman who had accompanied a team from that state to the Little League World Series in Williamsport made the mistake of bringing the youngsters to a Penn State practice. Paterno went ballistic, angrily shooing them all away. He later apologized, but the incident spoke to his mania and focus.

Linebacker Shane Conlan, who would go on to become an All-American, remembered what seemed to be an insignificant play during a practice in his freshman year. Wide receiver Kevin Baugh had feigned an injury after the snap. When Conlan stopped to check on his teammate's condition, Baugh dashed past him into the clear for a touchdown reception. Though Paterno was conducting a drill on an adjacent field, he had seen what happened.

"[Joe] comes running, yelling, 'You stink, Conlan! You'll never play here! Get off the field! You quit!' I've never been so nervous. I thought I was going to have my locker cleaned out," Conlan said.

When Penn State loses—or worse, doesn't play up to his expectations—Paterno can make things miserable. Disappointing defeats and seasons invariably are followed by an uptick in the workout rigors. For all his talk about molding well-rounded students, Paterno's practices can sometimes be so long and intense that weary players can barely drag themselves back to their rooms, let alone hit the books.

A typical week for a Paterno team begins on Sunday when he and his coaches break down game tapes and began devising a game plan for Saturday. On Monday, the tapes are reviewed at meetings of the various position players and their coaches. Tuesday, when the game plan is implemented and full-pad workouts begin, can be brutal depending on Paterno's mood and goals. On Wednesday, players practice for at least 90 minutes and attend additional meetings. Thursday is more of the same, with the intensity ratcheting up. Then on Friday, there is a walk-through, a bus to a State College hotel if Saturday's game is at home, and another team meeting. The schedule for Paterno and his assistants, of course, is far longer and more detailed and could best be characterized with a two-word description: nonstop work.

Potential players whose only experience with Paterno came during recruiting visits to their homes, where the coach has had few peers in his ability to charm parents, are sometimes shocked when they arrive on campus.

"I remember telling my mother, 'This guy's too nice to be a football coach,'" running back Charlie Pittman remembered. "Boy was I wrong. Once you're on campus, you see the real coach come out. He laid down the law.... I couldn't believe it the first time I heard him."

Pittman's experience was typical. The usual arc of a player's emotional relationship with Paterno over the course of an undergraduate career moves from awe to hate to respect to love.

His rules are rigid. Players are supposed to look sharp, behave, be prepared, be humble, be attentive, and be early. They should be clean-shaven, have a neat haircut, and never wear a hat indoors. They should remember they are college students—no matter how heavy their workload gets—and not just football players. They should never use their favored status as athletes to extort any favorable treatment. They should be attentive to their class work. They should not step onto the practice field unless they are willing to give it everything they have.

Trey Bauer, a linebacker in the mid-1980s, remembered his coach's reaction when Bauer fell short in several of those areas during his early days at Penn State. Bauer was a North Jersey kid, the kind of brash big-city boy who snickered at Central Pennsylvania and his coach's old-fashioned ways—in short,

Bauer was the kind of youngster who reminded Paterno of himself in 1950.

Bauer would later become a star, but when he arrived in State College, he had a bad attitude and a bad haircut. For one Sunday meeting, Bauer, who had been kicked out of study hall a few days earlier and had been drinking the night before, showed up tardy, his long hair spilling out of the baseball cap he wore.

"There was a collective gasp from the team as I came in," Bauer recalled, "and Joe started screaming at me. I saw him after the meeting and he told me, 'Here's the deal: I've had it with you. You'll never play at Penn State. I will give you your unconditional release. I'll call any coach you want in the country and try to get you into another school. You might as well transfer because you'll never play here.'"

Chastened, Bauer apologized to his coach, cut his hair, never showed up late to a meeting again, and became an outstanding defender on the Nittany Lions' 1986 championship team.

When he has earned the respect, trust, and devotion of his players, Paterno can be as encouraging as he is critical. Within the confines of their relationships, he seeks to know his players personally, to understand what they need, where they come from, how they are motivated. He remembers their younger siblings, their parents, what their mother fed him on recruiting visits. And for a man whose routines are so entrenched, he can be remarkably accommodating.

Harry Hamilton, a Penn State defender on the 1982 champions, once suggested to his coach that the training table needed some soul food.

"Within a week there were pigs feet and candied yams," said Hamilton, an African American. "A man like Joe Paterno [could have said], 'No, you don't suggest how I should run a football team.'"

Paterno often makes an extra effort with black players, understanding that some come from troubled backgrounds. State College is not an easy adjustment for them, and they might need more shepherding than white players from prosperous two-parent homes in affluent suburbs.

He often enlists his wife to help tutor athletes, black and white, in English and literature. When Bob White—who would be a defensive end on the 1986 champions—came to Penn State, he was concerned about making it academically. Paterno assured the small-town Florida kid he'd get the help he needed.

"I didn't grow up where around the dinner table you talked about your experiences in college because no one in my family had gone to college," White said. "[The Paternos] lived up to their word. Sue tutored me in English. She would work with me on papers I would write for classes. We would read books and discuss them and compare notes, whether it would be *A Tale of Two Cities*, *Moby-Dick*, or *The Adventures of Huckleberry Finn*. I never heard about them when I was a kid."

White not only graduated on time—he also went on to earn a master's degree in counselor's education.

The demands on Paterno's time and the size of the rosters has made it nearly impossible, but he tries to monitor his players' academic progress personally. In one-on-one encounters, both planned and unplanned, that invariably is the first topic he raises with the youngsters.

"I always told Joe when kids were having trouble, and he always backed me," said Don Ferrell, Penn State football's academic advisor for decades. "When kids weren't performing academically, he'd look at me and say, 'Did they flunk?' I'd say,

'Yeah,' and he'd take care of them. I never had to go out on a limb and do something against my character or integrity."

That attention to academics was more than lip service, and it was reflected in the school's graduation rates, statistics cited as often in Happy Valley as Paterno's five unbeaten seasons. By the mid-1990s, Penn State was graduating nearly 90 percent of its athletes while the Division I average was less than half that.

But just as he is seldom satisfied after practices or games, Paterno often feels that he should have done more to help those players whose lives after Penn State wouldn't be as successful as Bob White's life.

In the summer of 2004, Paterno was stunned to learn that Kevin Baugh, a gifted punt-returner and wideout on his first national championship team, had been murdered during a drug dispute in Massachusetts.

Baugh had been drafted but never played in the NFL. He moved from job to job until, not knowing where else to turn, he came back to Happy Valley in 1993. He told Paterno he'd had drug problems but was clean and needed a job. His coach helped him land a football position at a school in Utah. When things didn't work out there, Baugh's problems resurfaced and worsened.

"To this day," Paterno said, "I feel like I could have done something else.... Kevin had a broken family. He was trying to take care of his sister. He was trying to take care of a lot of things that he didn't have the resources for. I think the NCAA has to realize that there are some kids who, when they decide to go to college and play football, [are] forsaking some responsibilities."

Perhaps the things former players recall most vividly about their coach and his rules and regulations are the ones that involve dress—on and off the field.

When NFL players who have signed multimillion-dollar professional deals and played on Super Bowl teams eventually return to visit Paterno, his greeting often begins with, "Take that hat off. Didn't I teach you better than that?" At a 2004 pep rally in Rec Hall, as he sat with his team on stage, Paterno kept signaling to one of the youngsters onstage to remove his hat. As Nittany Lions players convulsed with laughter, the offender looked baffled at the coach's frantic hand signals. It turned out he wasn't a player, but rather a student helping out during the ceremony.

Paterno's mother was obsessed with making sure her children wore clean, well-pressed clothes at all times, so Paterno came by his interest in grooming naturally. He also got some reinforcement from his high school football coach.

In 1943, Zev Graham, a good friend of Yankees outfielder Snuffy Stirnweiss, took some of his Brooklyn Prep football players to a World Series game at Yankee Stadium. Though Paterno, a Dodgers fan, had always despised the American League champions, he found himself drawn to their professional-image and attitude—symbolized in his mind by their clean white pinstriped uniforms and polished black shoes.

"[Coach Graham] said, 'Now watch how the Yankees walk.' And sure enough, DiMaggio and those guys walked with a little swagger," Paterno recalled. "He said, 'Look at their shoes.' I said they were nice—I didn't know what he was talking about. The Cardinals came out. He said, 'Now look at the Cardinals shoes.' Every Yankee had polished shoes. They were all polished. The Cardinals had scuffed-up shoes, some of them didn't have the same length in their pants, the whole bit. He said, 'The Yankees are different.' You know, they had the pinstripes and the whole bit. And I think that's something that we try to do."

At Penn State, Paterno's teams would wear black shoes, short white socks, plain white pants, nameless blue or white uniform tops, and white helmets that once the numbers were removed in the 1970s contained only a narrow blue stripe. As other teams constantly altered their appearance, incorporating new and more popular colors and adornments, Penn State retained its drabness.

"A lot of people ask me about the lousy-looking uniforms that we have," Paterno said. "But you see us on TV and you say, 'Hey, Penn State is playing.' And your wife says, 'How do you know it's Penn State?' And you say, 'Look at the lousy uniforms.'"

Privately, the coach believed that a team needed symbols and that there was no room for individuality in football. It was why he disdained end-zone celebrations and taunting. Penn State players knew a gesture, even one as subdued as a raised arm, could win them a spot on Paterno's bench. "Act like you've been there before," became one of Paterno's most quoted maxims.

For him, the way his players acted and dressed said something about them and gave them a shared bond, a unique identity. "We're conservative, and we like team people," Paterno said. "We're not looking for flashy people. I think people every once in a while need symbols to reinforce those sentiments."

Penn State would wear its uniform uniforms throughout the 1960s and 1970s, even as America brightened considerably, shedding off the colorless residue of the conformist 1950s with a tie-dyed enthusiasm. At first derided as unimaginatively vanilla, the Lions' outfits developed a new cachet during the retro craze that began in the 1990s. Suddenly square had become hip.

So entrenched had the sartorial simplicity become that in 1985, the Nittany Lions players asked if they could remove the Orange Bowl patch from their uniforms for that game with

Oklahoma. The request was denied, but it was clear that they had gulped the coach's Kool-Aid.

"Even that little orange was too flashy," remembered Tom Shuman, a Penn State quarterback in the mid-1970s.

Paterno himself had a uniform. At practices, he wore a plain gray sweatshirt, brown khakis with the cuffs rolled up, white socks, and black spikes. On game days, depending on the weather, the outfit could change from blazer and tie to parka, or windbreaker, to shirtsleeves and tie, or even an occasional sweater and tie. But he rarely coached a game without his trademark rolled-up cuffs.

The habit developed simply enough. Sue got tired of paying to dry clean her husband's game-day dress pants—the cuffs were typically mud-splattered from all his sideline pacing. So she suggested that he roll them up. He did and even though he later switched to cheaper khakis for game days, the habit persisted.

The same reasoning applied to his footwear. Mud-dirtied and damaged were the dress shoes he originally wore as a Rip Engle aide. It was better to ruin a pair of spikes. Soon Paterno's wardrobe, like that of his team, became part of the legend.

"Nobody paid attention," he said about the uniforms, "until we started winning games."

And at no time would more attention be paid to Penn State's wardrobe than in the chaotic run-up to the 1987 Fiesta Bowl.

• • •

Todd Blackledge, Curt Warner, and several other key players graduated in 1982, so it was time for Paterno to recycle and build another team that could contend.

"I've always tried to put us in a position where we're building toward a team that could be a contender for a national championship," he said. "Sometimes it works. Sometimes it doesn't. It takes a while. We don't get rich quick. We don't take junior-college kids. We try not to take kids that don't belong here.… I have just felt, 'Let's do it the right way. Let's be solid. Let's build.' And if we're not good enough this year, at least we're not making sacrifices on the future in order to win X number of games this year."

The Nittany Lions went 8–4 in 1983, but the following season ended a string of 13 consecutive bowl appearances when the team slipped to 6–5. But in 1985, Paterno had another unbeaten regular season. That 11–0 team was thumped, ironically, by bad-boy Barry Switzer's Oklahoma 25–10 in another battle between the No. 1 and No. 2 teams, though this one occurred in the Orange Bowl.

The 1986 season would be Penn State's 100th in football. Expectations were high for a team that had two-thirds of its letter-winners returning, including 15 fifth-year seniors.

The defense, with linebackers Shane Conlan and Trey Bauer, would be solid again. Tailback D.J. Dozier had proved himself a more-than-capable successor to Warner. And Blair Thomas was there to fill in. The only question mark was the passing game. Though quarterback John Shaffer had lost only one start since junior high, throwing the ball was not his forte.

The 1986 season dawned with Penn State ranked No. 6. Schedules were made so far in advance that it was difficult to predict their relative strength from year to year. Texas A&M, for example, could be a beast when scheduled and a pussycat when the game finally rolled around.

While a strong schedule had helped in 1982, it seemed that 1986's opponents would be weaker and thus a worry for an independent team dependent on the polls for recognition. The 1986 Nittany Lions would beat just one ranked opponent during an 11–0 regular season, a groundbreaking 23–3 win at No. 2 Alabama on October 25. Bryant was dead by then, of course, but that marquee victory catapulted the Lions into the No. 2 spot in the polls. They would stay there until the January 2 Fiesta Bowl matchup with top-ranked Miami.

• • •

The 1986 season would be the high-water mark for football independents. Miami and Penn State became the first two to finish a regular season ranked first and second since Army and Navy four decades earlier.

But the lure of television money was opening a new era, one increasingly dominated by conferences. Over the next decade and a half, newly expanded and realigned leagues would proliferate everywhere as schools proved surprisingly willing to sacrifice tradition and independence for a fatter paycheck.

But in 1986, with no attachments to any bowl, Penn State and Miami found themselves in the midst of a buyer's market. As the two top-ranked teams, they could wait for the right offer. Since it couldn't come from one of the New Year's Day bowls, each of which still had conference commitments, a secondary bowl would have to step up. The 16-year-old Fiesta Bowl in Tempe, Arizona, did just that.

With NBC's backing, the Fiesta offered to double its payout to $2.4 million a team. Just as importantly, it agreed to move to January 2. Free from the New Year's Day bowl traffic, the Fiesta Bowl could have a prime-time audience all to itself.

And in Miami and Penn State, the Fiesta and NBC had a central-casting pairing of two perfect antagonists. The dramatic contrast in the two programs would make for must-see TV. Overall, 52 million viewers—a Neilsen rating of 25.1—would watch the game, both of which are college sports records that still stand a quarter-century later.

The Nittany Lions, with their white-bread uniforms, run-heavy offense, holier-than-thou coach, and high graduation rates, were portrayed as the white-garbed heroes.

Miami, hailing from the cocaine capital of the 1980s, were prone to trash talk and wild end-zone celebrations. With players whose names seemingly were as likely to appear in police reports as sports pages, the Hurricanes were the villains in black—or, in this case, camouflage.

As All-American wideout Michael Irvin proudly pointed out, the Hurricanes were ranked No. 1 "by the AP, UPI, and FBI." While their strutting, taunting style was off-putting to many, there was no denying the talent on Coach Jimmy Johnson's squad. In addition to Irvin, they had several names that would soon be making splashes in the NFL, including Vinny Testaverde, Randy Shannon, Winston Moss, Bennie and Brian Blades, Jerome Brown, Jeff Feagles, Alonzo Highsmith, and Winston Moss.

The two coaches also fit neatly into this desert morality play. The stone-haired Johnson could be as brash and flashy as his players. And if everyone hadn't yet known about Paterno's reputation, they learned that week when *Sports Illustrated* named Penn State's coach its Sportsman of the Year for 1986 and put him on its cover. Inside, Rick Reilly's glowing appraisal painted Paterno as the sport's last white knight.

"In an era of college football when it seems everybody's hand is either in the till or balled up in a fist, Paterno sticks out like a clean thumb," Reilly wrote. "His standard of excellence is so season-in, season-out consistent it borders on the monotonous… win ten, eleven games; send off another bunch of future doctors, lawyers, and accountants…when talking trash is hot and shaking hands before the coin toss is not…when it takes a paralegal just to make out the sports page, we need the guy in the PhotoGray trifocals more than ever."

Johnson apparently was one of the many coaches who resented Paterno's preachiness. He also couldn't have missed the way that some of Reilly's criticisms of the college game appeared to point to Miami.

When Johnson was asked during Fiesta Bowl week if he intended to recommend that the NCAA adopt some sort of overtime system, the sarcasm oozed from him like excess hair gel. "I could do it," he said, "but I think it would have more clout if St. Joe proposed it."

Two years later in his autobiography, Paterno returned the sarcasm, firing back at the Miami coach for failing to control his renegade team, especially during Fiesta Bowl week. After all, he wrote, those players "were representing the University of Miami and supposedly higher education."

As much as Johnson and his Hurricanes appeared to savor their public personas as villains and bad boys, they also genuinely disliked Penn State, whose "goody black shoes image" they were eager to scuff.

"We played for the national championship on September 27 [a 28–16 home victory over defending national champ Oklahoma]," said defensive tackle Dan Sileo. "As far as we're concerned, Friday's game is just the end of the season." When Jerome Brown was asked what he thought of D.J. Dozier and John Shaffer, he said, "I think they're nothing."

Because Miami's stars were predominantly black and Penn State's team was overwhelmingly white, race entered into the pregame discussions adding spice to an already intriguing matchup. The media's portrayals only tended to bolster prevailing stereotypes.

Bowl week began with controversy, and the tone seldom eased. Not long after the Nittany Lions arrived in sunny Phoenix wearing jackets and ties, at least a dozen Miami players deplaned in camouflage fatigues. Immediately the message was imparted that they were renegades, and this was war.

Camouflage aside, the Fiesta Bowl war had been waged from a safe distance...until a midweek steak fry that had been intended as a way to let opposing players get to know each other. This time it would be a Penn State player—punter John Bruno—who would ignite an incident some have since termed "the Tempest in a T-Bone."

Both teams had been asked to present a humorous post-meal skit, and Bruno delivered Penn State's. He talked about Johnson's infamous helmet of hair. Then he and a teammate struck some Heisman poses. The Hurricanes construed Bruno's routine as disrespecting Johnson and Vinny Testaverde, that year's Heisman recipient.

But Bruno made things worse when he indelicately joked about the two teams' racial differences, noting that at Penn State, "We even let the black guys eat with us once a week at the training table."

By then the Hurricanes were fuming. Some stripped off their sweatshirts to display more camouflage, as if they were provoked Clark Kents revealing themselves as Supermen. Brown told Johnson the players wanted to leave. The coach insisted they stay until the skit ended. When it did, he marched the team out of the room en masse and back onto their buses.

Paterno must not have known of Bruno's plans—given his natural-born cautiousness, he surely would have disapproved.

While Johnson attended the meal with his team, however, Penn State's coach did not, preferring to use the time for game preparations.

Many of the stories about the incident focused on Miami's departure and not what precipitated it. "People trash us because we all left together," Johnson said. "But Joe Paterno didn't even attend."

Paterno did not get drawn into the controversy. But in his autobiography, he would call Miami's actions that day "disgraceful."

Seventeen years later Fiesta Bowl president John Junker, who was there, defended the Hurricanes. "[Penn State's disrespectful actions] never got reported," Junker said. "I always thought that was a little unfair. Miami definitely got the rough end of the deal."

(Sadly, within six years, Bruno would be dead from cancer, and Brown was dead from injuries suffered in a car crash.)

The battles didn't end there. On game day, when Penn State players got off their buses and headed for their locker room, some Hurricanes impeded their way. Paterno stepped between them. The taunting continued on the field where several Miami players ran through lines of stretching Nittany Lions, a clear and deliberate breach of football etiquette.

Though Penn State was a seven-point underdog, Paterno believed if his team could confuse quarterback Vinny Testaverde, it could win. He and Jerry Sandusky devised new zone coverages, some of which dropped back eight defenders. So confident was Paterno in the Lions defense that when they won the opening coin toss, the coach chose to kick off.

Miami's offense was clearly superior to Penn State's offense. Alonzo Highsmith ran through the pass-conscious schemes with ease. But turnover after turnover by a confused Testaverde kept it close. The Hurricanes led 10–7 in the fourth quarter. Then Testaverde misread yet another coverage and Conlan intercepted him, returning the pass to the Miami 5. Dozier, who ran for 99 of the measly 162 yards Penn State amassed that night, scored with 8:13 to play, and the Nittany Lions were on top 14–10.

It would again come down to a fourth-and-goal, which Miami faced at Penn State's 10-yard line. Eighteen seconds remained when Testaverde took the snap. The Miami quarterback frequently telegraphed his intended targets, and this time he was fixed on Brett Perriman. Linebacker Pete Giftopoulos stepped in front of Perriman and made the interception. The new defensive schemes had worked. It was Testaverde's fifth interception.

And Paterno's second national championship.

13

IT MIGHT SOUND RIDICULOUS NOW, 20-plus years further into Paterno's seemingly endless reign, but after the Nittany Lions' second national title, Penn State administrators began to ponder a future without JoePa.

The importance of those considerations was quickly made clear to them. In 1988, two years after the Fiesta Bowl triumph, Penn State went 5–6, losing to several of the Eastern schools—Rutgers, Syracuse, West Virginia, Pitt—that earlier in the decade had been victory fodder. It was the first Paterno team to finish below .500, the first losing season at Penn State in a half-century.

How quickly the sky had begun to fall. Paterno was getting older. He'd be 65 in 1991. What would happen when he left? Who would be the face of the university? Who would maintain the traditions? Who would keep the cash flowing?

If the administration's first instinct was to panic, Paterno's was to push down on the accelerator, toughening up his already tough practice routines and team rules.

"Joe beat the crap out of us that winter," linebacker Andre Collins said. "We had to get up at 5:30 in the morning, which is something we had never done. We had to trudge through the snow for team aerobics.... Then after that we would have to wear a collared shirt to the dining hall. Joe just laid down the law. It was collared shirts. You had to wear socks. There were no Walkmen allowed in the football facilities. I just remember that being an awful, awful winter. By 3:30 in the afternoon, you were sleepy and starting to fear that next morning."

Not unusually, Paterno—who had won his 200th game in 1987—had offered some hints that he was nearing the end, an assessment he had made before and would again. Though decades of those false forecasts never brought him any closer to actual retirement, the coach apparently derived some comfort in predicting he'd be able to do it in three, four, five years.

Penn State president Bryce Jordan, who had succeeded John Oswald in 1983, was worried. Paterno couldn't go on forever. Either time or the torments of coaching eventually would wear him down. Then what? The school had grown dependent on the riches football accrued. That couldn't be jeopardized. They had to look for some security. It was time to rethink the possibility of joining a conference.

Penn State had remained an uneasy independent in a rapidly changing college sports landscape. New super-conferences and their television deals were at the heart of the changes. Television money expanded some leagues (the Big Eight and Pac-8), created some (the Big East), and killed others (the Southwest Conference). Notre Dame, with its national following, could command a network contract as an independent, but Penn State and the dwindling number of independents had no such clout.

The Big Ten had always seemed like a logical landing place. Central Pennsylvania, in its attitudes toward life and sports, tended to lean more Midwestern than Northeastern. And the university itself shared numerous attributes with Big Ten members. Like all save Northwestern, it was a public institution.

Like most, it was far removed from any large city. Massive Beaver Stadium was in line with the conference's outsized facilities. All had sizable student populations, leading roles as research institutions, powerful political connections within their states, and similar academic visions.

Whispers about a possible Big Ten move had surfaced as far back as the 1970s. President John Oswald was a Minnesota native. When he was head of the University of Kentucky in the 1960s, he had sought to upgrade that school's academic standing, and the Big Ten was his model. So when Paterno's Eastern league plans succumbed, Oswald, and later Bryce Jordan, began to nudge Penn State westward.

Sometime after the jarring 1988 season, the nudge became a push. Jordan contacted Big Ten officials, meeting secretly with Illinois president Stanley Ikenberry, who headed the Council of Ten, a group comprised of the presidents of the member institutions.

"[Jordan said], 'We think we've got to begin to plan for the post-Paterno era because, you know, Joe's not going to be around forever and he's getting up in years,'" Ikenberry recalled in a 2009 interview.

There were sizable hurdles. Rec Hall, which held fewer than 9,000 spectators, wasn't up to the standards of a Big Ten basketball arena and would have to be replaced. And then there was geography. State College was 276 miles east of the closest Big Ten school, Ohio State. It was one thing for Paterno's football team to fly charter to East Lansing or Madison in the fall, but it was quite another for Iowa's swim team to travel to State College in February. The closest airport that could accommodate large aircraft was in Harrisburg, which was 100 miles away. As summed up by Indiana basketball's coach Bobby

Knight when he learned of the proposed merger, "Penn State is a camping trip."

What really propelled the negotiations forward was the Big Ten's desire to add some of the East's television markets. Philadelphia, for example, was the nation's fourth largest television market. And in the populous corridor that stretched from Washington, D.C., to New York, there were millions of TV viewers and pockets of Penn State interest.

Though Paterno supported the move, he stayed in the shadows. If he had affixed his nationally prominent face to the proposal, the union would have been more difficult. Big Ten athletic directors weren't likely to welcome with open arms a new rival who could so easily upset the long-established balance of power. Plus, Paterno engineering a move whose rationale, no matter what was said publicly, was principally financial would have seemed beneath a coach so famously antimaterialistic.

Knowing that and sensing their opposition, Ikenberry, his fellow presidents, and conference commissioner Jim Delany kept the ADs and coaches in the dark throughout the negotiations. Paterno, meanwhile, was an active participant. As the talks intensified, he and Jim Tarman visited Illinois to talk personally with Ikenberry and to assure him and his fellow presidents that the conference's concerns would be addressed.

By the end of 1989, at a Council of Ten meeting in Chicago, the presidents made an informal decision to invite Penn State. When the media learned of it, the news touched off a firestorm in Big Ten athletic departments. Angered that they hadn't been consulted and wary of the impact Paterno's powerhouse program might make, some went public with their unhappiness, including Michigan athletic director and football coach Bo Schembechler, who would phone Paterno and call him "a sneaky little son of a bitch."

"It might be an interesting addition," the volatile Schembechler said. "I don't know how they will fit in. But you don't add someone to the conference and not consult the people from athletics. That was the most ridiculous thing I've ever seen done. I, and most of the other athletic directors in our conference, resent the way it was done, and if I offend some presidents, that's too damn bad. The time has come that if they want to take over, they'd better consult the people who know what the hell is going on. They did it because of the friendship they have with each other. One president probably said, 'Hey, I'd like to play in your league,' and the other president said, 'Come on over and do it.' That's about how much research went into that decision."

Penn State, of course, accepted the invitation and when the formal vote came in 1990, seven Big Ten presidents voted to approve the 11th member. Though the individual tally was never revealed, it was widely believed that Michigan, Michigan State, and Indiana were the dissenters.

The Nittany Lions' first conference football game wouldn't take place until 1993, but other sports would begin play sooner. The league's familiar name, though no longer numerically accurate, would not be changed.

• • •

Paterno's fingerprints, as Schembechler recognized, were all over the move, though officials on both sides continued to paint it publicly as primarily an academic decision. Jordan spoke of the 11 schools' "similar academic mission and structure." And Jim Delany called Penn State "a strong academic institution with world-renowned capabilities," a statement that was either hyperbole or proof that astounding progress had been made in the eight years since Paterno's 1982 plea to the trustees.

The deal's secrecy and the athletic directors' reactions ensured that Penn State would receive a harsh welcome on the field. What particularly annoyed some Big Ten coaches and athletes was the assumption that Paterno's Nittany Lions would waltz in and dominate. Pennsylvania lieutenant governor Mark Singel didn't help when he said, "What it means to Penn State fans is this: They can make plans to attend the Rose Bowl in the very near future." That quote found its way into locker rooms across the Midwest.

The anti-merger sentiment was strongest at Michigan where, as 1993 drew nearer, players were forbidden even to utter the words "Penn State." "We have to say 'the other team' or 'the 11th school,'" explained Wolverine running back Jon Ritchie.

Penn State's decision also prompted a further shakeup in Eastern football. In 1991, a version of the conference Paterno had envisioned a decade earlier took shape in more modest form. With prospects for an Eastern super-conference DOA, the Big East that year decided to add a football component. It incorporated Miami, Temple, Virginia Tech, West Virginia, and Rutgers, although the latter four were for football only.

Paterno, who would be 66 when Penn State played its first Big Ten game, had been hungering for a new challenge. Now he could guide his team to a Rose Bowl, the only one of the four traditional New Year's Day bowls he hadn't yet won. He dove into the big new pond instantly. Now indicating that he had no retirement plans, even when he hit 70, the coach started exercising more vigorously, lifting weights, and dieting. He had aides videotape every televised Big Ten game and added them to his off-season workload. "I go to sleep watching those games," he said in 1992.

There was a burst of fresh air on campus, too. In 1993, ground was broken for a new 15,700-seat arena that would be named for Bryce Jordan. Across Curtin Road, Beaver Stadium was expanded yet again. An upper deck was added to the north end zone, increasing seating capacity to 93,967.

Two thousand more fans than the upgraded stadium could officially accommodate filled it for Penn State's first Big Ten game, on September 4, 1993. Forty-three years after his arrival, the old coach found himself unusually nervous. "I went into the game with a little bit of anxiety," he said. He needn't have worried. His Nittany Lions made a sparkling debut, accumulating 504 yards of offense in a 38–20 victory over Minnesota.

A new era of Penn State football had dawned and with it came problems that certainly differed from the widespread perceptions of Paterno's program.

Wide receiver Bobby Engram had been the offensive star versus Minnesota. A year earlier, he'd been suspended after he and teammate Rick Sayles were implicated in an off-season burglary. That same year defensive back Brian Miller had been arrested and charged with cocaine possession, and four players—including Sayles and O.J. McDuffie—were involved in a well-publicized bar fight.

In the wake of those ugly incidents, a *Centre Daily Times* editorial noted that Penn State football's image had been tarnished. And as was the case whenever Paterno's players were linked to trouble, the coach's critics cried hypocrisy.

ESPN football analyst Beano Cook, the ex-Pitt sports information director and a burr in Paterno's side, said, "Penn State gives the impression that its kids walk out of chemistry class and say, 'We only have 16 credits this fall, let's play football.' My only resentment is those holier-than-thou statements, those self-serving statements. I don't get mad at Miami because they don't try to represent themselves like Penn State does. Penn State is no different than Miami, Michigan, Texas. It's a business. Notre Dame is no different. It's money."

It was hard to argue with that last assessment. Between 1996 and 2000, the six largest conferences—which in 1998 would join with Notre Dame to form a Bowl Championship Series, as close to a playoff format as Paterno was ever likely to get—took in $373 million from televised football.

As budgets and revenues grew, football coaches became CEOs responsible in most cases for the financial welfare of entire athletic departments. Losing couldn't be accommodated or tolerated for long, so those who failed were fired quickly and the winners found themselves in demand, moving like mercenaries from school to school, lured by multimillion-dollar contracts.

Penn State would long keep Paterno's earnings a state secret. But in 2009, as a result of a lawsuit filed by a Harrisburg newspaper, a judge ruled that because Paterno would be collecting a state pension, it had to be revealed.

Paterno's base salary and bonuses topped $1.03 million, a figure that did not include any of the outside compensation— sneaker contracts, radio and television shows, etc.—that coaches at big-time schools generally earned. Though he was still underpaid by the standards of other big-name coaches, he had come a long way from the $20,000 he made in 1966. "No coach is worth that kind of money," Paterno said of the million-dollar plateau.

• • •

Even though he was closing in on 70 and had a staff that, like the Nittany Lions' stadium, grew constantly, Paterno continued to function as a de facto offensive coordinator. And the offense he and Fran Ganter oversaw in 1994 would be the best in Penn State's history.

That talented unit would average 520 yards and 47.8 points a game—both national bests—setting 14 school records along the way. It featured five All-Americans—Engram, quarterback Kerry Collins, guard Jeff Hartings, tight end Kyle Brady and tailback Ki-Jana Carter—four of whom would be first-round NFL picks, with Carter the No. 1 choice overall in 1995. Their numbers were so mind-boggling that they were generating the kind of individual attention Paterno had always tried to deflect.

"He used to yell at us and call us a bunch of fatheads," Collins recalled. "That was his favorite term for us. We were a bunch of fatheads because we were getting a lot of accolades and putting up a lot of points with a very prolific offense. So every day in practice he would ride us. He never once conceded that we were any good.... That's part of what makes Joe Joe, that kind of attitude. He always wants you to stay humble and always wants you to be hungry."

The seeds of Paterno's most recent unbeaten team were planted early in the 1993 season when he replaced quarterback John Sacca with Collins. The Nittany Lions would lose consecutive games to Michigan and Ohio State, then turn invincible. They won their final five games, including a 31–13 rout of sixth-ranked Tennessee in the Citrus Bowl, and finished as high as No. 7 in the polls. They'd gone 10–2 overall and 6–2 in their first Big Ten season.

In 1994, it wasn't really fair. Penn State would kick off the season with a 56–3 rout at Minnesota. The Nittany Lions would surpass 50 points six times and 60 twice that season. A comeback victory at Michigan in Week 6 vaulted the Lions to the top of the polls.

That prime-time win over the No. 6 Wolverines sparked off another of those spontaneous campus celebrations—or, depending on your point of view, riots—that seemed to happen whenever the Nittany Lions won a big road game on national television. This time 10,000 students roared across the darkened campus like a whirlwind. Near midnight, a small pack broke into Beaver Stadium and tore up sod, which infuriated Paterno.

The field was back in shape on October 29. With revenge on their minds and a record home crowd of 97,079 in the stands, the Lions pounded Ohio State 63–14. A year earlier, they'd lost their first Big Ten matchup with the Buckeyes and been derided by the winners as "pussies" who couldn't compete in their new league.

Before that rout began, unbeaten No. 2 Nebraska had defeated No. 3 Colorado. Penn State undoubtedly recognized it needed an impressive win, and there were those who felt its sizable margin of victory over the Buckeyes reflected that understanding.

That was an unusual charge to be making about a team coached by Paterno, who had developed a reputation as perhaps the lone college coach unwilling to roll up the score. Blowouts tended to impress poll voters much more than hard-fought squeakers, so it was hard to blame any coach for seeking additional points. When asked afterward if his team had piled it on, Paterno refused to discuss it or anything related to the polls. His reticence could have been a tacit defense of players who wanted to pulverize Ohio State for their earlier comments. "You guys can talk about it," he said. "You have papers to sell. I don't have to talk about it, and I'm not going to."

As imposing as that Ohio State score might have appeared, it failed to move some poll voters. Penn State stayed at No. 1 in the CNN and *USA Today* rankings but dropped behind Nebraska in the AP voting. A week later, a Paterno decision to not run up the score would cost his team their top ranking and, ultimately, a third national title.

Following the emotional wins over Michigan and Ohio State, the Nittany Lions experienced a letdown at Indiana.

Still, they had a comfortable 35–14 advantage against the 5–3 Hoosiers midway through the final quarter when Paterno pulled his starters. He had done so scores of times before in one-sided victories, explaining that it was concern for his team as much as for the opponents that motivated the move.

"What I owe my team is to make sure everybody plays and works hard and I have an opportunity to play them. I think that for me to take some kids who look forward to playing on a Saturday and not play them when I think the game is in control because I want to make sure that we win by X number of points so we can preserve a place [in the polls] would be irresponsible," he said in a run-on explanation unworthy of an English major.

As fate would have it, Indiana scored a pair of touchdowns in the last three minutes, the second on a Hail Mary pass as time expired. Hoosiers coach Bill Mallory, who had been an outspoken critic of Penn State's inclusion in the Big Ten, curiously ordered a two-point conversion try, although it was meaningless. The try was successful, and the final tally in the Lions' victory was a misleading 35–29.

The bulk of poll voters, of course, saw the final score and not the entire game. Since the Cornhuskers had romped Kansas 45–17, they leapfrogged Penn State to the top of all the polls.

A week later, extraneous circumstances and a close call again prevented Penn State from moving up. At Illinois, a hotel power outage disrupted Paterno's carefully planned game-day rituals. Sleepy players had to climb up and down steps and eat hastily ordered pizza instead of the healthier brunch fare that had been planned. (All 50 of the pies white-bread Penn State ordered, by the way, were plain.)

Illinois jumped out to a 21–0 lead against the sluggish Lions. With 6:07 to play and down 31–28, Penn State got the ball on its own 4-yard line. But Collins completed all seven passes on a 96-yard drive that produced a 35–31 victory, the first time any Paterno team had overcome a deficit as large as 21 points.

There would be no change in the polls then or after both Penn State and Nebraska finished out the regular season with two victories.

Ironically, Penn State's new affiliation kept it from another matchup between the first- and second-place teams in the Orange Bowl. As Big Ten champs, the Lions would meet No. 12 Oregon in the Rose Bowl, and Nebraska would face No. 3 Miami at the Orange Bowl.

Again, their championship dreams were beyond their control. If the Lions were going to win a third national crown in 12 years, they would have to beat Oregon, hope their old Hurricane antagonists could take care of the Cornhuskers, then pray that they got more poll votes than Miami.

In Pasadena, Carter ran 83 yards for a touchdown on the first play of Penn State's 38–20 New Year's Day triumph. But Nebraska also won 24–17. Paterno had his New Year's Day grand slam, but the Cornhuskers had a win over a higher-ranked foe and the title. The fact that Nebraska's popular coach Tom

Osborne had never won a national championship didn't hurt his team's chances in the final voting.

It was the fifth time a Paterno team had won all its games but not a championship. There had been a single loss in 1982 and 1986. But now, with two trophies back in State College, Paterno's complaints were tepid though elegant in their simplicity. "If I could do anything about it, I'd do it," he said. "If I could rant, scream, and yell and get people to change their votes, I'd do it. But it's over. I don't think it was fair. I think we were as good as anybody. I wouldn't say we were better than Nebraska, but we were as good."

Penn State still would benefit greatly from its first visit to the Rose Bowl in 71 years. Researchers long ago had disproved the notion that athletic success translated into increased contributions. But a 2000 Western Economic Association International study would find that the lone exception was a major bowl victory. The Nittany Lions Club reported a major uptick in donations following that Rose Bowl. Applications and season-ticket requests also increased, the former by an estimated 15 percent.

The Big Ten had its benefits. But there remained those convinced that Penn State's move made it far more difficult to win a third title or to fulfill its coach's more noble ambitions. "While it certainly put the university into a higher academic league, it kind of ended the Grand Experiment," said a longtime Penn State beat writer. "To compete at the Big Ten level, with no Marylands, Syracuses, Temples, and Pitts to fatten the record, they had to turn down the quality-control button and ramp up the 40-yard dash times."

Penn State did get better athletes, many of them black, in the 1990s, but why they got them has never been established.

The school's graduation percentage hovered between the low and high 80s. There still have been no NCAA probes. While there was a bump in the amount of trouble his players got into, Paterno always insisted many of the offenses were relatively minor and likely wouldn't even have surfaced in his early days.

• • •

In his seventies as the end of the millennium approached and with a pair of national championships under a belt that would have fit him in 1950, Paterno was aging better than his Grand Experiment.

Little change had resulted from all the coach's sermonizing about the dangers of freshman eligibility, the need for booster controls and a workable playoff system, the financial and academic help many disadvantaged athletes required, and the insidious influence of commercialism. As the 21st century loomed, the abuses that had marred college football since its 19th century inception clung stubbornly to the game.

Elsewhere, graduation rates remained abysmal. Academic scandals—like those that would rock Minnesota, Georgia, and Tennessee—were commonplace. The seasons kept getting longer, and television's demands were more numerous. Schools shuttled from conference to conference seeking bigger paydays. Boosters continued to make noise and trouble. Players earned as much ink for problems off the field as accomplishments on it. The term *student-athlete* dripped with irony.

Paterno could talk all he wanted, but college football at its highest level wasn't about producing well-rounded individuals, if it ever had been. It was instead a desperate continuous search for money, enough money to sustain a successful program, build appealing facilities, and support the rest of the athletic department.

Division I football, in particular, had become a major commercial enterprise, one buttressed by tax breaks, wealthy donors, television money, and corporate sponsorships. And Penn State eagerly joined the treasure hunt.

The 1990s would witness an unparalleled growth in college athletics. By the end of the decade, fueled by the kind of galloping commercialism Paterno had long decried, collegiate sports would be a $3.5 billion enterprise. Even Paterno, his idealism leavened by pragmatism, would yield to the new realities.

By 1999, Penn State's football program was by some measures the nation's fifth largest, generating revenue of $25.4 million. With expenses of $8.8 million, that left a tidy profit of $15.6 million. The athletic department, which had an endowment of $18 million, spent $5.5 million annually on scholarships—twice as much as it spent on academic aid for its brightest students.

Football games had become marketing devices aimed at attracting and appeasing alumni, boosters, and donors. The logos of major corporations like Pepsi, AT&T, and Nike adorned Beaver Stadium. Penn State would collect nearly $9 million from its football seating plan that, based on the amount of their tax-deductible payments, rewarded boosters with the best seats. And the stadium's signature view of Mount Nittany—which had infatuated broadcasters and cameramen on football telecasts for decades—was being obscured by one more expansion.

Paterno by then had allowed, reluctantly, the ubiquitous Nike swoosh to mar his team's famously pristine uniforms. He had also become a shareholder in various Penn State–related enterprises, including a web site for coaches and a retirement village. And he had an enormous new office in a new $14.7 million football building that included a two-story weight room, spa, and 180-seat auditorium.

"We've tried to stay as pristine as we could," Budd Thalman, an associate athletic director, said at the time. "But the bottom line is…in order to fund some of these programs, you have to begin to make compromises."

No longer was the proper recipe for college sports the Grand Experiment's mix of athletics and academics. The new formula for success was being able to strike a balance between athletics and entertainment. Schools like Penn State tried to keep sports an essential part of campus life while at the same time using them to appease alumni, boosters, and donors—and attract applicants and subway alumni, to boot.

"We're very mindful of maintaining that balance," said president Graham Spanier, who succeeded Joab Thomas in 1995. "I think we come as close as anybody to upholding the principles that have provided the foundation of intercollegiate sports. We want people to come to our events, have a good time, and feel proud. We want them to tune in and watch us on television. To the extent people are proud of Penn State athletics, we believe that enhances the image of the university."

• • •

On October 13, 1995, Paterno would become a grandfather for a first time when daughter Diana gave birth to Brian Andrew Giegerich. Over the next decade and a half, the number of Paterno's grandchildren would grow to 17. Two weeks before Brian's birth, four games into Paterno's 30th season as head man, he marked his 500th game as a coach at Penn State. The Nittany Lions ended that season with a 9–3 record, another top 20 ranking, and an Outback Bowl victory over Auburn in Paterno's record 27th postseason game.

He was not just a grandfather now but the game's elder statesman, its wise sage, its decorated hero. A four-time winner of the American Football Coaches Association's Coach of the Year Award, Paterno in 1991 became the first active coach to receive the National Football Foundation's Distinguished American Award. Brown, Gettysburg, and Allegheny College would present him with honorary degrees in the decade. He was the friend of U.S. presidents and had more clout than his university president.

In 1997, work began on the $34.4 million Paterno Library on Penn State's main campus. Having helped to raise almost $15 million for its construction, Joe and Sue, two lifelong bookworms, beamed at the groundbreaking. The Paternos donated $3.5 million in 1997 to endow faculty positions and scholarships and to support a pair of building projects.

Then in the second game of the 1998 season, a 48–3 thrashing of visiting Bowling Green, Paterno became just the sixth coach in NCAA history to win 300 games. That team also finished 9–3, received a top-20 ranking, and won an Outback Bowl.

"It's always seemed to me that Paterno is one of those special men," noted author David Halbertsam said. "He brings honor to what he does. He's one of those rare people who has lived up to the ideals of intercollegiate athletics. He's one of those people who has a mystique that you hear about and then it turns out to be true. There have been no flaws in his career."

He did, of course, have flaws. He was beginning to snap more at reporters in news conferences and at assistants on the sidelines. Even he would admit that he had scaled back some of his youthful dreams to accommodate later realities. He had done the best he could, but he was not perfect. His humanity would be confirmed for the nation during an ABC telecast of a Penn State–Rutgers game in 1995.

In the final minute of a game his team led 52–34, Penn State's backup quarterback—future Lions assistant Mike McQueary—had thrown a 42-yard touchdown pass to a wide receiver.

Had it been any other team, any other coach, there would have been no doubt that this was a case of rolling up the score. But this was St. Joe. He wouldn't commit such a sin, would he? The broadcasters weren't sure, but they immediately and correctly surmised that Rutgers' coach Doug Graber would be upset.

A camera focused on Penn State's sideline, where a somewhat chagrined-looking Paterno appeared to be asking Fran Ganter, his chief offensive aide, "What happened?"

Seconds later, when the two head coaches met at midfield for the postgame handshake, Graber said something inaudible. Paterno turned and responded as he exited the field, "Ah, bullshit! Bullshit!" ABC's microphones were close enough to pick up the expletives and, at his weekly news conference three days later, Paterno was asked if he wanted to apologize.

He began by explaining that the play had been designed as a short pass but that McQueary had noticed Chris Campbell break free and instinctively hit him.

"I shouldn't have to apologize for Mike doing what he has been coached to do," Paterno said. "I feel very, very bad about the [swear] words. I would not want my kids to have to listen to a national figure go on television and say what I said."

His kids, of course, listened to "a national figure" every time their father spoke to them. Paterno—all "bullshit" aside—had long been a national icon. *The New York Times* called him the "nation's most revered college football coach," and no one could have argued. He was so instantly recognizable, his integrity so universally unquestioned, that he frequently had been urged to try politics. A 1988 Harrisburg *Patriot-News* poll found that Penn State's coach was the state's most popular figure by a better than two-to-one margin.

The son of an FDR Democrat, Paterno was a longtime Republican. His political views, according to brother George, could probably best be described as moderate—conservative on foreign policy and financial issues but for the most part socially liberal. Those views in swing-state Pennsylvania, coupled with his off-the-charts recognition factor, could have made him a formidable candidate. He frequently was approached about supporting local or statewide candidates or even about running himself for Congress or governor.

President Gerald Ford, himself a former college football player, said that when he was in the White House he tried to convince the coach to seek a Pennsylvania congressional seat. "But he was so dedicated to Penn State and young people he turned me down," Ford remembered.

In the 1980 Republican presidential primary, Paterno supported George Bush over Ronald Reagan and developed a friendship with the future 41st president and his future-president son. Eight years later, Paterno surprised everyone when he agreed to give one of the seconding speeches for the elder Bush's nomination at the GOP convention in New Orleans.

As Pennsylvania Democrats disapproved and Republicans defended his decision, Paterno explained that he had agreed to do it because he felt Bush was "a great man" and because his own father had always urged him to try to make a difference.

"It's a vehicle for a private citizen to have an impact in a political campaign," he said. "I want to have an impact on something I think is important. My dad always had a feeling that he owed something to this country, that he wanted to give something back."

The speech was a standard boilerplate endorsement, sprinkled with several sports references, a joke or two, and a surefire applause line in defense of Bush: "I'll be damned if I'll sit still while people who can't carry George Bush's shoes ridicule him."

Four years later, Paterno introduced the then-president at a Penn State campaign rally, and he would do the same in 2004 for President George W. Bush.

Also in 2004, Paterno's son Scott, who was an attorney, ran for Congress in the state's 17th District. Paterno accurately forecast his defeat at the hands of popular Democratic incumbent Tim Holden. Paterno didn't come to his son's campaign headquarters on election night. Speculation suggested that he stayed away because he didn't want to be a distraction or because he sensed a loss was inevitable. The real reason, given Paterno's history, was probably far more practical. His 2004 team was in the midst of another losing season and the 77-year-old Paterno just couldn't spare the time.

14

IN THE FALL OF 2001, a team of craftsmen raised a small semi-circular wall outside Beaver Stadium's north entrance. On one of the masonry construction's three sides were affixed the words: "Joseph Vincent Paterno: Educator, Coach, Humanitarian." Another panel contained plaques listing the results of the 415 games he'd coached between 1966 and 2000. And on the last there was this quote: "They ask me what I'd like written about me when I'm gone. I hope they write I made Penn State a better place, not just that I was a good football coach."

Finally, late in October, the shrine was completed when an enormous 7-foot, 900-pound bronze statue of Paterno—built to last at least as long as the flesh-and-blood model—was dropped into place. With rolled-up cuffs, spikes, his tie wafting in imaginary winds, and an index finger thrust hopefully into the air, it was a precise representation of the coach during a familiar Beaver Stadium ritual, the pregame entrance.

And yet something wasn't right.

The statue had a physical uprightness that didn't match the coach's anxious stoop. The smiling expression lacked his thoughtfulness. And whatever it was that animated the fidgety coach, that had for decades propelled him from the darkened tunnel into the pregame sunlight on autumn Saturdays was missing.

That wasn't the sculptor's failing. There has always been something hidden, some wellspring of resolve and introspection that, despite a lifetime in the spotlight, Paterno kept concealed. Most see him, rightly, as an admirable amalgam of character, caring, coaching genius, and cleverness. But anyone convinced they know Joe is bound to be surprised. After all, he has been surprising people his entire life.

He surprised high school and college opponents who couldn't see beyond his limited physical abilities. He surprised his parents by choosing coaching over the law. He surprised his older colleagues when he wasn't afraid to question and challenge them, even as a rookie coach. He surprised his friends and himself when he turned down a million dollars and the NFL. He has repeatedly surprised the sports world by refusing to retire, even when it seemed the only right thing.

And then there was perhaps the greatest surprise of all, the astonishing 2005 season. At 78, battered relentlessly during an unprecedented run of losses, he proved that his critics were mistaken, his bosses were unnecessarily anxious, and his obituaries were extremely premature.

If the statue had been sculpted after that remarkable season, its raised index finger might instead be wagging in the faces of his detractors, scolding them for thinking they understood Joe Paterno.

• • •

That Paterno statue was set in place the week after his 324th victory, a 29–27 triumph over Ohio State that made him the winningest Division I-A coach ever. Few noticed at the time, but even as the old coach was being carried off the field on his players' shoulders, there was trouble in the air.

The front edge of a completely unexpected storm, one that soon would threaten Paterno's job and legacy, had first appeared in Happy Valley 23 months earlier, just 55 days before the new century dawned.

Until then, nothing in the otherwise sunny 1990s had hinted at its arrival. Paterno's Nittany Lions went 97–26 in the decade, played in a bowl every year (winning seven), finished ranked in the top 25 all 10 seasons, and drew record crowds to Beaver Stadium. In their first seven years as a Big Ten member, they'd won 41-of-56 conference games and had managed a league title and a Rose Bowl victory.

The black clouds appeared from out of nowhere late on the sunny homecoming afternoon of November 6, 1999. Penn State was 9–0 at the time, ranked No. 2 in the polls, and with a stout defense anchored by players who would be the first two picks in 2000's NFL draft—LaVar Arrington and Courtney Brown—this edition was in position to become Paterno's sixth unbeaten team, maybe even his third national champion.

The Nittany Lions led 23–21 with less than 2 minutes to play when Paterno, facing a fourth-down at Minnesota's 33, decided to forego a field goal try and punt. The kick rolled into the end zone, and the Gophers took over at their own 20 with 1:50 left.

There was time for a long drive, but, for some still inexplicable reason, Coach Glen Mason ordered a Hail Mary pass on first down. Quarterback Billy Cockerham, on the move as he avoided a rush, hurled the ball downfield. At Penn State's 34, wideout Ron Johnson leaped and caught it.

Two incompletions were followed by an Arrington sack of Cockerham that pushed the ball back to the 42. Now it was fourth down with seconds remaining. Again Cockerham evaded the rushing defenders. His hurried throw bounded off a Gophers wideout and then a Penn State defender before landing in the outstretched arms of Arland Bruce, a Minnesota senior who until that moment had 14 career catches.

At Penn State's 15, there was time for nothing but a 32-yard field goal attempt by Don Nystrom, who earlier had missed an extra point. The snap was good, and rising just above Arrington's outstretched arms, Nystrom's kick sailed high and true. Minnesota had an improbable fate-aided 24–23 win. "I've never gotten over that game," Arrington would say 10 years later.

The aftermath had a similar effect on Penn State football. A program that for a half-century had been climbing steadily higher stumbled and fell. And it would be another six years before it regained its equilibrium.

The stunned 1999 Nittany Lions would lose their next two games (to Michigan and Michigan State), finishing the regular season a disappointing 9–3. They fell to 13th in the rankings, though they did manage a 24–0 shutout of Texas A&M in an Alamo Bowl that was their sendoff for retiring defensive coordinator Jerry Sandusky.

In 2000 Penn State went 5–7, including an embarrassing home loss to Toledo, and a kind of irritated buzz developed in the shadows. Already there were signs that something was different, that perhaps age and time had at last overtaken the coach. Running back Larry Johnson, the son of a Paterno assistant, was bitter after the Toledo loss. "The teams that play us know what we're going to run," Johnson said in a postgame analysis that helped fan the flames of dissent. "They can pull out the tapes from '92 or '93, and we run the same offense.... The system is too predictable. It's been around too long."

Was he implying that the coach also had been around too long? If so, he wasn't alone. The unease, now concentrated on Paterno, increased when the 2001 season began with four unnerving defeats that sandwiched the jarring tragedy of September 11. Penn State would go 5–6 that year. A second straight losing season was something that hadn't happened in State College since 1931–32. Now nerves were on edge. The angry cyber-chat and the whispers about Paterno grew louder.

• • •

Personally, things hadn't been going much better for Paterno.

In the fifth game of that 2000 season, one of his players, freshman Adam Taliaferro, had been seriously injured trying to tackle an Ohio State runner. Taliaferro's fifth cervical vertebra burst on impact. He could not move from the neck down.

Eventually, Taliaferro was transported to a rehabilitation hospital in Philadelphia. Paterno, perhaps reminded of his son's fall, took the injury hard. He would call it one of his worst coaching experiences. Though until then he'd had little personal contact with the stricken freshman, Paterno flew to Philadelphia every Thursday to visit Taliaferro. Occasionally, some players or Sue, bearing homemade cookies, accompanied him.

Ever the coach, Paterno preached to Taliaferro. He assured him that he was going to get better in time to lead the Nittany Lions out of the tunnel for the 2001 home-opener. It seemed an impossibility, especially to Taliaferro. "He was so positive and I was like, 'But Coach, I can't even walk,'" Taliaferro said. "He told me not to worry, to keep working hard and thinking positive, and I'd be walking again and leading us out of the tunnel when we played Miami."

On September 1, 2001, as a Beaver Stadium crowd of 109,313 stood, cheered, and tingled, Taliaferro, wearing street clothes and moving haltingly but steadily, emerged from the tunnel alongside his coach. Though he never played again, Taliaferro would continue to improve, return to school, earn his degree, and with Paterno as one of his references, gain admission to Rutgers Law School. He graduated in 2008 and now is a Philadelphia attorney.

"He was so important to me," Taliaferro said of the coach. "And even now, 10 years later, he asks whenever I see him if there's anything he can do to help. That's the kind of coach he is. That's the kind of person he is."

Taliaferro's ordeal brought Paterno to tears, something son Jay said he hadn't witnessed since the coach's mother died. Florence Paterno passed away at 92 in 1988, outliving her husband by 30 years. Following her death and after George's tenure as Penn State' radio color commentator concluded in 1999, the Gold Dust Twins slipped apart.

George, a gadfly and a barfly, had attended several Nittany Lions games in the intervening years, but the two brothers rarely had time for the long walks and long talks they once enjoyed. They'd once been inseparable—brothers, best friends, and backfield mates at Brooklyn Prep and Brown. However, while they looked alike and while their Brooklyn-trained voices were eerie echoes, they had always been different. One was the model of stability. The other was eccentric and free-spirited. Life had brought them to two different places. One followed his destiny. The other—a New York City cop, a Merchant Marine Academy football coach, a broadcaster, a bachelor—chased his dreams and never quite caught them.

During his radio broadcasts with play-by-play man Fran Fisher, George appeared to take a good-natured delight in zinging his brother and his play-calling. If it bothered Joe, he was too savvy to say so publicly. Joe had seldom complained about critical coverage, so he didn't gripe about George's comments on the radio or those in his 1997 book, which revealed a more human portrait of Penn State's coach than any of the Paterno hagiographers.

He could not, however, resist a tiny dig in the blurb he wrote for George's book. "My brother tells me that the book is 80 percent good, 10 percent bad, and 10 percent his own personal observations," Paterno wrote. "That's fine with me."

Sue Paterno, who tried to monitor everything written and said about her husband, had become his reputation's bodyguard. She occasionally would tell Paterno about one of George's second-guesses. "I get asked if [Sue] ever considers spiking my coffee with arsenic," George said in 1994. "I say, 'Nah, she knows there's no viciousness in my comments.' But if I'm at the house for postgame lasagna, sometimes she won't give me an extra serving."

In June 2002, at the age of 73, George died shortly after suffering a heart attack. Paterno was devastated. He hadn't realized his brother, who still lived in New York, had been so ill. "I just wish I'd known," he said, as if he'd have found a way to make a difference. A *Sports Illustrated* writer would later note that, "[When] George died, a little piece of Joe died, too."

• • •

There was a welcome and brief break in the storm in 2002 when Penn State won nine of 13 games, its three regular-season losses coming by maddeningly narrow margins. Yet even then there were enough disturbing events on the periphery to foster additional concerns about the future of the program and, more specifically, its coach.

The Lions won their three opening games that season. They trailed Iowa in Game 4 at 35–13 before rallying and sending the game to overtime. Iowa scored a touchdown on its first overtime possession and Penn State was driving to answer. But Tony Johnson was ruled out-of-bounds on a third-down catch that would have produced a first down. Replays, which Paterno could see on Beaver Stadium's video board, revealed that the call was wrong and that the receiver had been safely in bounds. When a fourth-down pass failed, Penn State had been beaten.

Afterward, a clearly frustrated Paterno chased down referee Dick Honig to complain about that call and another in overtime that had gone against his team. Catching up with the official in a Beaver Stadium tunnel, the coach grabbed him by the back of his striped shirt to get his attention.

As infuriating as the bad call was, Paterno's unusual and physical reaction only confirmed what a lot of observers—many of them Penn State loyalists—already believed. The coach was so old and so frustrated that if a change wasn't made soon, he would embarrass himself further. He had always griped to officials on the sideline. But to chase one down and grab him? This didn't fit the image of St. Joe. Neither did his response when he was asked if he regretted his actions.

"Why?" Paterno asked. "What did I do? I did not make contact with him. I just tried to stop him because he was running ahead of me. I was running into the locker room and grabbed him by the shirt and said, 'Hey, Dick, you had two lousy calls.' I said two guys on the other side of the field had two lousy calls. I am not allowed to do that?

"I was behind him. I didn't want to knock him over. He is a good official. My gripe wasn't with him. My gripe was to make sure he understood that I thought there were a couple of guys who made bad calls."

Two weeks later, virtually the same thing happened in a loss at Michigan. Penn State was driving for what could have been a game-winning field goal when again a Johnson catch was nullified by an out-of-bounds call. Once again, replays showed that he was in bounds. Once again, the Lions would lose in overtime. And once again, Paterno would be furious. Though he didn't confront any officials this time, he wouldn't allow his players to talk to the media. Later, Larry Johnson would say what all his teammates felt: "We got hosed."

Penn State accepted a Capital One Bowl bid to play Auburn. But a few weeks before that game, starting freshman cornerback Anwar Phillips was accused in a campus sexual assault and suspended. The suspension, however, wouldn't take effect until the new semester started in mid-January. When Paterno played Phillips in the January 1 loss, the howls of protest echoed across the state. The player eventually was acquitted of the charge and rejoined the team. But the reaction had been so fierce that Spanier was forced to declare that no player facing a suspension would again be permitted to play.

The level of negativity rose significantly in 2003 thanks to events on the field and off. In the summer before that season, center E.Z. Smith was suspended for a year after receiving two underage drinking citations in the same week. Offensive lineman Tom McHugh was cut when he was cited for public drunkenness and harassment after allegedly striking a female student. Punter Jeremy Kapinos was nabbed for underage drinking and disorderly conduct.

Alcohol-related misconduct was a problem on most U.S. campuses, and at some point those problems infected most athletic teams. But the number of incidents and the way they contrasted with long-held perceptions of Penn State football made these occurrences more noteworthy.

Although by then Paterno's shepherding had helped produce scores of scholars, doctors, lawyers, teachers, entrepreneurs, and executives, this unusual run of misconduct was seen as symptomatic of the coach's diminished control and capacities.

Record-wise, the 2003 Nittany Lions would be his worst team ever. They beat Temple, Kent State, and Indiana—a traditionally weak trifecta—but no one else. When the unprecedented season ended mercifully after a 41–10 butt-kicking at Michigan State, Penn State was an almost unimaginable 3–9 overall and 1–7 in the conference.

In the midst of that mess, there would be more problems. Tony Johnson had been stopped while driving erratically. A test revealed his blood-alcohol level to be 0.136, far above Pennsylvania's legal limit of 0.08. Several days later, Paterno appeared to defend the player during a news conference. "It will get blown out of proportion because he is a football player," the coach said. "But he didn't do anything to anybody."

So many alarm bells went off at groups like Mothers Against Drunk Driving and Students Against Drunk Driving that Paterno was forced to apologize.

Just weeks before the Blue-White game in April 2004, three returnees who were expected to play crucial roles in what Paterno hoped would be a revival—quarterback Michael Robinson and defensive linemen Ed Johnson and Matthew Rice—were involved in an ugly brawl at an ice rink.

Meanwhile, wideout Maurice Humphrey, perhaps the one deep threat Paterno had, was expelled for assaulting two female students.

Each incident raised new questions and new complaints. The besieged coach was alternately angry, frustrated, and guilty. The anger and frustration stemmed from reasons that were apparent. But the guilt ran deeper. It grew out of a concern that perhaps he hadn't involved himself enough in the lives of these players.

"I have a handful of kids that are immature jerks who have been spoiled by their families," he said. "They're not bad kids and they're going to be all right, but sometimes you'd like to have a baseball bat to wake them up."

The ill winds intensified to hurricane force in 2004, lashing at Paterno who, in his late-life torment, had come to resemble Shakespeare's King Lear. As one writer pointed out, "[Paterno was] an increasingly tragic figure moored on the storm-wracked heather of his legend."

By the fall of 2004, he was the hot topic in any discussion about Penn State football. He was too old, too stubborn, too conservative, and/or too shortsighted to recognize he was doing long-term harm to the program he'd built. The critics were students, alumni, sportswriters, fans, professors, administrators, and radio callers.

The state of Penn State football and Paterno's responsibility for it had produced an unusually volatile atmosphere at State College. Everyone had an opinion about what was wrong. Some of the explanations were mystical. (The football gods were angry because the latest stadium expansion obscured the signature view of Mount Nittany.) Some were practical. (They miss Sandusky.) Most zeroed in on Paterno. (It was his staff or his son—Jay was an offensive assistant—or his age.)

And those who had no explanation had a joke, often about the supposedly addled coach. "Did you notice last week?" *Miami*

Herald columnist Greg Cote wrote. "Poor Paterno coached the entire game with his left blinker on."

There was serious sharper-edged criticism, too. "Penn State football is supposed to matter," said Ryan Jones, a 1995 graduate who could have served as a spokesman for the discontented. "We boast proud traditions and a coach and a program that still stand for things most programs and coaches don't. But we're not relevant any more, and life was a little bit better when we were."

Through it all, a core of supporters remained numerous, vocal, and steadfast. They still believed Paterno had earned the right to leave at a time of his own choosing. Jim Meister, the president of the State College Quarterback Club, was typical. "[Paterno] deserves to be handled differently than anyone else," Meister said. "He put Penn State on the map. No matter where you are, if you mention Penn State, people will say, 'Isn't that where Joe Paterno is?'"

As the coach increasingly turned aside questions about his job status, attention turned to Penn State's administrators and trustees. The trustees, most of them Paterno loyalists, avoided the unpleasantness as best they could. They insisted the football coach's future was not even on their agenda. "The board is behind Joe," said chairwoman Cynthia Baldwin, "but his future is not a board issue." In other words, if he were going to be fired or somehow shoved aside, it would be up to president Graham Spanier and athletic director Tim Curley. Few believed they had the clout to do either. But at some point they had to respond to the concerns. When they did, it was a head-scratcher.

In May 2004, Penn State rewarded the 77-year-old coach, then in the final year of his existing contract, with a four-year extension. If they thought that nod to stability would quell the raging storm, they were wrong.

All across the country, columnists and broadcasters reacted incredulously to the news, unable to grasp why Penn State would deal with its most pressing problem by postponing any decision. The feelings among many on campus were similar. "It's disappointing," Paul Morrison, one of the first Nittany Lions Club boosters to call for Paterno's replacement, said of the news. "I just haven't seen the performance on or off the field for the past handful of years. I was hoping to see a change of direction, someone new with more youth and energy."

While he couldn't do anything about his age, Paterno as usual had no problem summoning up additional energy in the face of a crisis. He attacked this latest and greatest challenge with his typical zeal. According to Curley, "Over the years, every time things started getting a little rough, [Paterno would] always be one of those guys who thrived on it. The rest of us would get gray hair and go crazy, and he's not like that. He's so competitive he seems to welcome the challenge."

This time among Paterno's solutions was a reshuffling of his coaching staff. Believing that there were too many demands on his time, he created a helper. He shifted longtime aide Fran Ganter into an administrative post, replacing his top offensive aide with Galen Hall. Paterno refocused himself on practices and on his relationships with players, monitoring more closely their performances on the field and in the classroom. Grooming policies would be strictly enforced, and anyone late for a meeting did so at his own peril. He announced a zero-tolerance for any new off-the-field problems. "He told us, 'That's it. Next incident, you're gone,'" quarterback Zack Mills said. "He was tired of it happening every other week. He's serious. The margin for error is gone."

And then his 2004 Lions went out and lost seven of nine games to open the season. Proud Penn State, Joe Paterno's Penn State, had lost 16 of its last 20 games.

• • •

As the "Joe Must Go" talk raged, a defiant Paterno remained on message about his team.

He had a defense with heart. And, as usual, he had great linebackers. But the offense, without any breakaway speed or deep threats, was positively anemic. Five times in 2004 Penn State would score seven points or less. In a painful-to-watch homecoming loss to Iowa, the Nittany Lions were beaten 6–4, their meager scoring output coming on two safeties. And yet whenever he was confronted with the ugly realities, Paterno continued to insist his team was "just one or two skill players away from being really good." To all but the coach, the assessment seemed simple-minded, wrong, and even worse, desperate.

Is this how nearly 40 years of excellence was destined to end? With a delusional coach? The Penn State nation was perplexed. Used to more stability than supporters of any other program in the nation, they didn't deal well with uncertainty. They had a million questions and no answers. They didn't want to callously cast Paterno aside, but couldn't he at least anoint a successor? He could say, "Look, here's my guy. I'm going to phase myself out over the next two or three years, and then I'll hand him the reins."

Those who said that didn't know the coach. Not only wouldn't he consider walking away or designating a successor, he wouldn't even tolerate such talk. Friends reported that anyone who dared suggest one of those options had been "cut out of his life."

Matt Millen, by then an NFL executive, contacted his old coach, thinking he might offer him some counsel. "You know,

Joe, it really isn't my business, but you should name a successor," he told him. "It doesn't mean you have to retire."

Paterno shot back, "Millen, you're right—it isn't any of your business."

During Paterno's weekly conference calls and interviews, questions about his status proliferated. One never knew how he might respond. He could be funny and self-effacing. When asked if he'd been moved to do any soul-searching, he said he might have done so "but I couldn't find my soul." He could be overly sensitive. One reporter who asked about Paterno's status was chastised for disrespecting him. He could be thoughtful. When asked how his literary-minded wife was dealing with the criticism, he said he and Sue were more likely to discuss the fact that Dante was gay. And he could also be angry or insolent.

"If you think I'm going to back out of it because I'm intimidated, you're wrong," he said early in the 2004 season. "If you think I'm going to stay when I think I'm not doing a good job, you're wrong.... We have to recruit some skilled people. I have said that before."

No matter the mood he adopted, he couldn't hide his frustrations. Once on his weekly radio show, when the stream of negative comments and questions finally got to him, he gave voice to them. "What can I tell you? We're frustrated," he told a caller. "You know, we're frustrated. Frustrated. You know how to spell it? F-R-U-S-T-R-A-T-E-D."

• • •

P-A-T-E-R-N-O was the overwhelming topic of conversation for homecoming alumni in the days before and after that Iowa debacle. Graham Spanier and Tim Curley couldn't avoid the talk. Realizing the angry tone was an accurate reflection of the mood on campus and beyond, they knew had to do something.

Having awarded Paterno a four-year extension six months earlier, they couldn't so soon afterward pull the plug on a legend. Their only hope to quell the rebellion was to convince Paterno to retire.

In the week after a 14–7 home loss to Northwestern left the Nittany Lions 2–7, the two administrators told Paterno they'd be dropping by his house "to discuss my future." There, they told him they wanted him to think about stepping down after 2005.

He didn't need to think about it. Paterno responded by telling Spanier and Curley what he'd been telling sportswriters all year. A turnaround wasn't far off. He wasn't going to abandon his program in its current state. He could fix things. Be patient.

Even if he had agreed to leave in a year, who would have succeeded him? Let the talk-radio hosts and columnists tout national names like Kirk Ferentz or Rick Neuheisel or Urban Meyer. When it came time to name a replacement, Paterno wanted to do things the way Engle had by promoting an assistant. That way he'd be promoting continuity, guaranteeing that everything he'd built wouldn't be jeopardized by some outsider's outsized ego.

But there was no clear-cut heir-apparent on staff. Among Paterno's long-time aides, Dick Anderson had failed as Rutgers' head coach and was in his mid-sixties himself. Galen Hall was the same age and had been fired at Florida. Jay Paterno was too young. He had a name that would insure continuity but, in the eyes of most Penn State diehards, not much else. Tom Bradley, Larry Johnson, and Ron Vanderlinden made more sense, but there was little to choose among them and each had drawbacks.

Spanier and Curley were stymied. They'd played their one hole card and had seen it trumped. "I just didn't think that was the way to do it," Paterno recalled about the meeting. "And I said, 'No, I don't want to do it that way.' I said, 'Let's see what we can get done this year.'"

• • •

The unrest was eased a bit by two season-ending wins over Indiana and Michigan State—which improved the 2004 Lions record to 4–7—and the news that Paterno might be getting some of the skill players he craved.

Happy Valley deserved its name, and its residents were uncomfortable being uncomfortable. "I know that in places like Philly or Chicago, sports fans tend to be more critical," former linebacker Bob Mitinger said several months before his 2004 death. "But up here, at least when it comes to Penn State football, we tend to always look ahead, always look for the positive."

Before the 2005 season got under way, they found it—a last-minute goal-line stand at Indiana had won that game and instilled some badly needed confidence. The switch to the more explosive spread offense against Michigan State had resulted in 37 points, 15 more than the powder-puff attack had managed against any other Big Ten foe. Michael Robinson, who would succeed Zack Mills at quarterback for his senior season, had multiple skills and the respect of his teammates, and at least two players with those much discussed attributes of agility and speed were en route.

Paterno wanted Derrick Williams, a speedy Maryland running back, kick-returner, and wideout who had been rated as the nation's top prospect by some scouting services. Paterno even sent Williams a three-page handwritten letter. Defensive coordinator Tom Bradley, meanwhile, had written 30 notes to Justin King, the Pittsburgh-area son of a former Nittany Lion and one of the premier high school cornerbacks. Their handwritten diligence paid off. Penn State landed both of the noteworthy talents.

But if speed and athleticism were the traits that Paterno and Penn State needed, revenge was what they truly desired. Everyone was determined to restore the Lions' badly tarnished image, to shut up the critics, snickerers, and doubters. No one felt stronger about that than Paterno himself. "Don't ever tell Joe he can't do something," George had said, "because he'll work harder than ever to make sure he does it."

At the Big Ten media day in Chicago before the 2005 season, Penn State was an afterthought. Few of the assembled reporters wanted to talk with the two Penn State players—Michael Robinson and linebacker Paul Posluszny—who had accompanied their coach. And the bulk of questions for Paterno concerned his retirement plans. When the traveling party returned to State College, they suddenly had a "them" to put against their "us."

Paterno gathered his team around him, let them know about this latest snub, told them no one believed in them, and recited Hamlet's soliloquy. It wasn't exactly vintage Knute Rockne, but it allowed the players to see that this 78-year-old who had suffered the slings and arrows of outrageous fortune was as passionate and determined as ever.

"He got up there and he started in with this 'To be or not to be' stuff," Robinson said. "Nobody was really sure what he was saying, but he told us we were going to stick together and that we weren't going to lose a game that season."

It was amazing how this 78-year-old man could keep generating and renewing energy and enthusiasm. So confident was Paterno of the 2005 team's success that in May he hinted to a group of Pittsburgh fans that he'd quit if he failed. 'If we don't win some games," he told a gathering of the Duquesne Club, "I've got to get my rear end out of here. Simple as that."

Why would anyone believe him? How many times, to use *Centre Daily Times* sports columnist Ron Bracken's phrase, had Paterno "[hit] the reset button on his retirement clock?"

When Penn State's freshman class arrived on campus late that August, Paterno asked to address them. "He was eloquent," Graham Spanier recalled. "He received two standing ovations. He's as engaged and determined as I've ever seen him. His passion for this season is great."

So was the passion of the players. Robinson and his wide receivers had worked out together, in private, throughout the off-season. Their bond would prove essential. Paterno, meanwhile, wanting to take advantage of the kind of athleticism he'd rarely before had in a Penn State quarterback, dispatched his offensive assistants to Texas. Vince Young, whose talents resembled Robinson's, would lead the Longhorns to a national title in the upcoming season, and Paterno wanted his aides to find out if Robinson could be utilized as effectively.

The coach continued to tweak his own contributions, as well. He eased back on the details and delegated more responsibility, especially to Hall and Bradley. He focused on Robinson, who played so spectacularly that people soon wondered why Paterno hadn't used him sooner.

Williams was loosening up defenses and giving ulcers to opposing special teams coaches. Justin King was shutting down top-flight receivers, and Paul Posluszny, Dan Connor, Tamba Hali, and Alan Zemaitis were tackling everything that moved.

On the field, the 2005 season would be the antithesis of 2004. They made big plays and timely plays. In a last-minute win at Northwestern, using a play they'd worked on in their private workouts, Robinson hit tight end Isaac Smolko on a key fourth-and-15 conversion. A nationally televised victory over Ohio State was punctuated by Hali's game-clinching sack of Buckeyes quarterback Troy Smith.

Suddenly, the student body was more excited and animated than it had been since the 1990s. Several hundred students had camped out in tents outside Beaver Stadium days in advance to get the best seats for the Ohio State game, a gathering the media quickly dubbed "Paternoville." Following that victory, the Nittany Lions were 6–0 and back in the top 10 for the first time in the new millennium.

A painful last-second loss in Ann Arbor would keep the Lions from competing for a third national title and would be the only blemish on an 11–1 season that ended with a triple-overtime win over Bowden's Florida State in the Orange Bowl.

More disciplinary problems, these involving E.Z. Smith again plus Dan Connor and defensive end Scott Paxson, couldn't dim the revival's glow. Paterno refused to gloat. Although, when someone leaked news of his meeting with Spanier and Curley, he was happy to confirm it.

Whoever the source was, it wasn't the old coach. By then, his relationship with the reporters who covered his team—many of them four, five, even six decades younger—had deteriorated to a historic low. "I can't trust you guys anymore," he told them. "I'm just being honest with you. It's no fun. I don't like you guys anymore."

And there were some who still didn't like the coach. During Orange Bowl week, Florida State had sent a player home after a 19-year-old woman had accused him of an assault in his hotel room. When asked about the incident, Paterno responded with remarks that women's groups across the country decried as flippant and insensitive. "It's so tough," he'd said. "There are so many people gravitating to these kids. [He] may not even have known what he was getting into. A cute girl knocks on the door, and what do you do? Geez, thank God they don't knock on my door.... But that's too bad. You hate to see that."

The old coach looked tired and beaten down after the long and dramatic Orange Bowl, which ran on until 12:58 AM. But as he broke down the game for reporters, he seemed to revive himself. And why not? This was a moment of great personal satisfaction. He'd proved the world wrong.

"We were so happy for him," Robinson said. "All those people wanted him to leave, and he stayed put and kept the faith. That's why he's been so great for so long. He knows what has to be done, and he does it."

• • •

He could have walked away after that moment of vindication. He would be 80 in less than a year. Penn State had risen to No. 3 in the polls and had come within 2 seconds of again being in the national championship discussion. He didn't, of course. And by then, anyone who expected he might have just hadn't been watching very closely. Joe Paterno wasn't going anywhere. Ever.

Bowden's son, Tommy, predicted that either his father or Paterno, and maybe both, would die on a football sideline.

His words proved nearly prophetic in 2006 when Wisconsin linebacker DeAndre Levy slammed into Paterno on the sideline during a game in Madison. A shinbone was fractured, and knee ligaments were shredded. Paterno had surgery and missed the Temple game. But he was back in the press box for a Michigan State win and an Outback Bowl victory over Tennessee that capped a 9–4 season.

Then in 2008, after an 11–1 regular season and a third Big Ten championship, Paterno underwent hip-replacement surgery on November 23. This time the 82-year-old coach was back in the press box for a New Year's Day loss to Southern Cal in the Rose Bowl.

Paterno's doctors were astonished at how completely the octogenarian had recovered from two serious operations. Soon he would even reclaim his familiar spot on the sideline.

After that New Year's Day game in Pasadena in 2008, Paterno's contract was set to expire. Inevitably, renewed speculation arose that Paterno would be stepping down. By now, the number of people who took any conjecture about Paterno seriously had diminished greatly. They were convinced he wasn't going anywhere.

Sure enough, on December 16, Spanier announced that Paterno had been granted a three-year extension. This time, as opposed to 2004, the news created little buzz. Curiously, this deal allowed either Spanier or the coach to alter its terms at any time, though anyone who believed the university president was brave enough to exercise that option was as naïve as the retirement speculators.

In 2009, Penn State went 9–4 and defeated Tennessee in a bowl game. When the season ended, Paterno said, "I can't wait for next year."

• • •

Paterno has a career record of 401 wins, 134 losses, and three ties for a winning percentage of .748 (ties count as ½ win and ½ loss).

In his 45 seasons as a head coach, he has had 38 winning seasons, one more than Bear Bryant. Based on the criteria used by the NCAA, Paterno holds the record for most victories by a

Division I-A/FBS football coach and is second only to Eddie Robinson's 408 victories among Division I coaches.

In November 2010, Paterno would become the first major college coach to win 400 games when his Nittany Lions overcame a three-touchdown deficit to defeat Northwestern. The huge Beaver Stadium crowd roared and chanted his name. Paterno stood unmoved on the sideline. Afterward, players lifted the old man onto their shoulders. "They had me up there before I knew it," he said. "I was hoping they wouldn't, to be very honest."

The milestones were so routine by now that his wife had not even planned to attend the game. But son Jay intervened. "[Jay said,] 'Mom, I hate to tell you, but it's kind of a big deal. Four hundred wins really hasn't been done at this level,'" Sue Paterno said.

Shortly afterward, Paterno said he intended to return in 2011, the final year of his contract. "We could be a pretty good football team next year," he said, an assessment so familiar that it could have been uttered before any of his many seasons, "and I'd like to be part of it."

His 45th head-coaching season, which had begun with a thumping in Alabama's heat, ended with an Outback Bowl loss to Florida and a mediocre 7–6 record. Before the bowl in Tampa, rumors popped up that Paterno was ailing again. Bloggers suggested he was waiting until after the game to announce his retirement. As always, he denied it all…and more vehemently as the questions persisted.

"Get off that thing, will you, for God's sakes?" he said during a bowl-related conference call. "How many times can I answer the same question? I must have answered that question 50 times. I've told you, I have not given it any thought. It does not bother me. It bothers you guys. I want to go down there and have a good football game, period. Can't you get that through your head? Right now, that's the only thing I'm thinking about."

But even his players weren't convinced. "Even though Joe said he's going to come back for another year, we don't know for sure," said tailback Evan Royster. "It's exciting for us to play like it's his last game. I think that's the mind-set of a lot of us."

Despite Paterno's earlier assurances that he'd be returning in 2011, the doubts were reasonable given the circumstances. It seemed a perfect time to step away. His entire family was in Florida with him. He could have gathered them at the podium after the game, made his announcement, and been done with it.

Leaving after 2010 would have provided a neat numerical punctuation mark for a career that began in 1950. He had 45 seasons as head coach. He had surpassed 400 victories. And for the Penn State program, which was about to embark on a touchy and controversial plan to rearrange Beaver Stadium's seating chart, his departure would have provided a fitting background for a new beginning.

But Paterno wasn't searching for the perfect ending, then or ever.

Ironically, it was his Outback Bowl coaching rival, 46-year-old Urban Meyer, who instead had revealed that he would be retiring. Meyers, whose buttoned-down demeanor, good looks, and consistent success often led to speculation that he might be Paterno's successor at squeaky-clean Penn State, was leaving for health reasons.

Everyone had a theory as to why Paterno has stayed. Maybe it was loyalty, dedication, hard-headedness, passion, inertia, fear, or delusion. Maybe he was waiting for the right time or the right successor. Perhaps he was holding out until son Jay was ready. Or maybe he was looking for the courage to do it, to admit his life's mission—his life, really—was over.

Nobody really knew. Because nobody really knew Joe Paterno. For a man who had spent six decades in the spotlight, who had been the subject of countless magazine pieces, documentaries, books, and newspaper columns, he remained largely unknowable. "I found it almost impossible to tell people what Joe Paterno was really like," writer Ronnie Christ said. "He has virtually no close friends but hundreds of acquaintances."

• • •

On a snowy day that winter, some of Paterno's unofficial acquaintances stood alongside his statue in the Beaver Stadium grotto. Earlier, some enterprising prankster had managed to remove the glasses from the coach's bronzed likeness, but these visitors didn't seem to notice.

They had come to State College for a campus tour with their daughter, a high school junior from Hagerstown, Maryland. While she was having coffee with a student guide, her parents had made their way to this isolated spot.

They were Maryland football fans. But if their daughter picked Penn State, they admitted, they could be converted. Although now middle-aged, they had heard about Paterno all their lives. Now they read the season-by-season plaques and the inscriptions on the walls. The husband posed for a photo with a raised arm draped around the sculpture's lofty neck.

"Maybe if Caitlin ends up here, I'll get to have a picture with the real Joe," he said. "If he lives that long."

"Oh, he'll live that long," his laughing wife said. "From what I hear, JoePa will never die."

At that moment, the real coach was not a half-mile away, at work in the office whose enormity embarrassed him. Spring would come soon to Happy Valley. The snow would melt, the hillsides would turn green again, and prospective students and their parents would visit more often.

And Joe Paterno would prepare for another football season.

BIBLIOGRAPHY

ARCHIVES

"History of Sport in America Course" by Ronald A. Smith, Student Papers on Penn State Athletics, Penn State University Libraries, Special Collections.

The Joseph V. Paterno Papers, Penn State University Libraries, Special Collections.

The Charles A. "Rip" Engle Papers, Penn State University Libraries, Special Collections.

The Coaching Life of Charles A. "Rip" Engle by Joseph Kugler and Robert Rangel, 1985, Kittochinny Historical Society Papers.

BOOKS

Coach: The Life of Bear Bryant by Keith Dunnavant, Simon & Schuster, 1996.

Joe Paterno: In Search of Excellence by James A. Paterson and Dennis Booher, Leisure Press, 1983.

Joe Paterno: Football My Way by Joe Paterno, Mervin D. Hyman and Gordo White, Macmillan Co., 1971.

Joe Paterno: The Coach from Byzantium by George Paterno, Sports Publishing, 1997.

Lion Country: Inside Penn State Football by Frank Bilovsky, Leisure Press, 1982.

The Lion in Autumn: A Season with Joe Paterno and Penn State Football by Frank Fitzpatrick, Gotham Books, 2004.

The Nittany Lions: A Story of Penn State Football by Ken Rappoport, The Strode Publishers, 1980.

No Ordinary Joe: The Biography of Joe Paterno by Michael O'Brien, Rutledge Hill Press, 1998.

Paterno: By the Book by Joe Paterno with Bernard Asbell, Random House, 1987.

Penn State: An Illustrated History by Michael Bezilla, Penn State University Press, 1985.

Playing for Paterno: One Coach, Two Eras: A Father and Son's Recollections of Playing for JoePa by Charlie and Tony Pittman and Jae Bryson, Triumph Books, 2007.

Road to Number One: A Personal Chronicle of Penn State Football by Ridge Riley, Doubleday & Co., 1977.

They Know Joe by Neil Rudel and Corey Giger, Altoona Mirror, 2010.

What It Means to Be a Nittany Lion: Joe Paterno and Penn State's Greatest Players by Lou Prato and Scott Brown, Triumph Books, 2006.

NEWSPAPERS
Allentown Call
Altoona Mirror
Centre Daily Times
Daily Collegian
Harrisburg Patriot-News
Philadelphia Daily News
Philadelphia Inquirer
Pittsburgh Post-Gazette
Reading Eagle